PROFITABLE PARTNERSHIPS

The Policy Studies Institute (PSI) is Britain's leading independent research organisation undertaking studies of economic, industrial and social policy, and the workings of political institutions.

PSI is a registered charity, run on a non-profit basis, and is not associated with any political party, pressure group or commercial interest.

PSI attaches great importance to covering a wide range of subject areas with its multi-disciplinary approach. The Institute's 40+ researchers are organised in teams which currently cover the following programmes:

Family Finances and Social Security
Health Studies and Social Care
Innovation and New Technology
Quality of Life and the Environment
Social Justice and Social Order
Employment Studies
Arts and the Cultural Industries
Information Policy
Education

This publication arises from the Industrial Development Programme and is one of over 30 publications made available by the Institute each year.

Information about the work of PSI, and a catalogue of available books can be obtained from:

Marketing Department, PSI
100 Park Village East, London NW1 3SR

PROFITABLE PARTNERSHIPS

A REPORT ON BUSINESS INVESTMENT IN THE COMMUNITY

Case studies from three British cities

Ian Christie, Michael Carley and Michael Fogarty
with Robin Legard

Policy Studies Institute
100 Park Village East, London NW1 3SR

The publishing imprint of the independent
POLICY STUDIES INSTITUTE
100 Park Village East, London NW1 3SR
Telephone: 071-387 2171 Fax: 071-388 0914

© Crown Copyright 1991

Published by permission of the Comptroller of Her Majesty's Stationery Office.

ISBN 0 85374 534 X

A CIP catalogue record of this book is available from the British Library.

1 2 3 4 5 6 7 8 9

How to obtain PSI publications
All bookshop and individual orders should be sent to PSI's distributors
BEBC Ltd, 9 Albion Close, Parkstone, Poole, Dorset, BH12 3LL.

Books will normally be despatched in 24 hours. Cheques should be made payable
to BEBC Ltd.

Credit card and telephone/fax orders may be placed on the following freephone
numbers FREEPHONE: 0800 262260 FREEFAX: 0800 262266

Booktrade Representation (UK & Eire)
Book Representation Ltd
P O Box 17, Canvey Island, Essex SS8 8HZ

PSI Subscriptions
PSI publications are available on subscription.
Further information from PSI's subscription agent
Carfax Publishing Company Ltd
Abingdon Science Park, P O Box 25, Abingdon OX10 3UE

Laserset by Policy Studies Institute
Printed in Great Britain by BPCC Wheatons Ltd, Exeter

Acknowledgements

The study on which this report is based was funded by the Inner Cities Directorate of the Department of the Environment. The content and the conclusions presented here are, of course, entirely the responsibility of the authors.

The report is the work of a team. Ian Christie edited the report and wrote Part I; Michael Carley carried out the fieldwork in Birmingham and wrote Chapter 7; Michael Fogarty was responsible for the Bristol study and for Chapter 8; the Manchester case study was carried out by Robin Legard.

Valuable advice and encouragement was provided throughout the project by a Steering Committee, to whose members we are extremely grateful:

Robert Charleston – Chairman (Inner Cities Directorate, DoE; on secondment from TSB Group)

Rose Albrow (formerly at The Industrial Society; now at the East London Partnership)

Stephen Batey (Inner Cities Directorate, DoE)

Penelope Clarkson (Business in the Community)

John Conder (Institute of Personnel Management)

Celia Hensman (Inner Cities Unit, DTI)

Amanda McIntyre (Confederation of British Industry)

Penelope Smith (Inner Cities Directorate, DoE; on secondment from the European Commission)

Marco Torquati (Association of British Chambers of Commerce)

John Uden (Action Resource Centre)

We are most grateful to the many interviewees from companies, voluntary agencies and public bodies who generously gave their time in the course of the study.

Contents

Executive Summary

1. Introduction

Since the early 1980s there has been a considerable development of business investment in the community in the UK. The concept of community investment embraces all forms of corporate support for the voluntary sector, community groups and partnership ventures involving the voluntary and public sectors.

2. The nature of company investment in the community

2.1 Community investment covers many forms of business activity and support for the voluntary sector and community groups. Traditionally the emphasis has been on donations to charitable bodies in cash and kind. However, numerous other methods of business involvement have grown in importance in recent years:

- financial support (project funding, 'soft' loans, matching grants, payroll giving schemes, donations to intermediaries for distribution in the community);
- sponsorship of community projects or events (including social and environmental sponsorship as well as the more familiar forms of corporate sponsorship for the arts and sports);
- donation of equipment, products and materials to community bodies;
- provision of staff time and expertise, for example through secondments, part-time assignments, volunteering and membership of governing boards;
- recruitment and training initiatives aimed at broadening opportunities for specific disadvantaged groups;

- education/business partnerships and related ventures with local schools and colleges;
- support for local enterprise promotion, for example through initiatives to increase local purchasing from small firms in the community.

2.2 The extent of business investment in the community has increased substantially over the past decade. In 1989 the estimated total for company contributions was at least £300m, excluding the value of gifts in kind: of this some £175m was in the form of charitable donations. However, the real level of community investment is certainly much higher, since many firms do not account comprehensively for non-cash support such as provision of staff time (pp 10-11).

2.3 In the 1980s there was a large increase in the promotion of business investment in the community. This was the result of a number of factors, for instance alarm in the private sector over the rise in unemployment and inner city disturbances in the early 1980s. Numerous agencies have emerged to promote greater involvement by companies in national and local action for community causes (pp 11-15).

2.4 Companies may become involved in the community investment field for reasons of self-interest as well as altruism and social concern. While 'philanthropic' motivation is very important to many firms and individual employees, there has been a growing emphasis among promotional agencies, voluntary bodies and companies on action based on 'enlightened self-interest'. Increasingly, companies, promotional bodies and the voluntary sector are seeking to become involved in initiatives that can provide benefits to the company as well as to the community. This is widely regarded as the key to recruiting many more companies into the world of community investment (pp 19-23).

2.5 Benefits for companies from investment in the community may emerge in the short and the long term. Short-term benefits may be more easily quantified: for example, improved recruitment and retention associated with schemes for pre-recruitment training for disadvantaged groups. Long-term benefits may be hard to quantify, but companies and community bodies alike identify a variety of advantages flowing to firms that become involved in the community (pp 23-28).

- long-term revival of economic activity in disadvantaged areas and consequent growth in custom and business opportunities for companies;
- the development of a pool of potential skilled employees in inner city localities through training initiatives and new recruitment policies focussing on local communities;
- maintenance and enhancement of company image and goodwill among local communities;
- improved employee motivation and retention, and an enhanced image for companies among potential recruits and customers;
- improved employee motivation and development of new skills through assignment to projects in partnership with voluntary bodies and community groups.

3. Good practice in company investment in the community

3.1 The review of activity in our three case-study cities reveals many positive examples of community investment by firms. Although cash donations are still the main item for many firms, other forms of investment are becoming well-established. There are no areas of activity that are the sole preserve of larger enterprises, and smaller companies can play an important role in the community.

3.2 There is widespread agreement among leading firms, promotional agencies and voluntary bodies on the key elements of good practice in community investment:

- the development of a statement of company policy on community investment that has board-level support, specifies areas for support and sets priorities, identifies aims and objectives, and provides a clear message to employees, shareholders and the wider community about the company's commitment (pp 36-39);
- commitment of resources to community investment as an integral part of the company's activity, to be managed like other mainstream functions, rather than as a marginal 'extra';
- involvement of all levels of staff in community initiatives;

- flexible allocation of resources between national and local initiatives, allowing effective targeting of particular local needs (pp 41-42);
- entry into networks and partnerships involving links with community bodies, other firms and public sector agencies, in order to pool resources, improve coordination of activities and information exchange, and bring a mixture of skills to bear on complex problems, especially in inner cities (pp 42-48).

4.   Overcoming obstacles to community investment

4.1 As well as general agreement on elements of good practice, there is also a broad consensus among firms, promotional agencies and voluntary bodies on the obstacles to the development of corporate investment in the community. The main problems identified are:

- relatively low levels of corporate expenditure as a percentage of pre-tax profits, and inadequate reporting of investment (pp 51-52);
- the failure of many firms to develop comprehensive policies on community investment and their reliance on ad hoc responses to requests from the community (pp 52-53);
- the need to raise managers' awareness of potential benefits and recruit many more firms into the culture of community investment (pp 54-60);
- the confusion felt by many companies over fragmentation in the voluntary sector, over public policy initiatives in the inner city and over the plethora of partnership ventures that have been established between private, public and voluntary bodies in recent years (pp 61,67-69);
- the need for more participation by local authorities and the voluntary sector in partnerships involving business in community investment, and for more emphasis on 'social regeneration' as well as physical and commercial development in urban renewal ventures (pp 65-67).
- the need, as seen by many companies and other bodies, for 'strategic fora' at local level to coordinate initiatives for community investment and improve information flows (pp 69-70);

4.2   Measures that may be useful in overcoming these obstacles include:

- more dissemination of guidelines on good practice for companies in relation to organisation, budgets and policy development for investment in the community (pp 52-53);
- further development of initiatives for increasing company contributions such as the local Per Cent Clubs operating in Newcastle and Sheffield (p 55);
- more resources for promotional and voluntary bodies marketing the message of company investment in the community, especially to smaller firms not yet involved (p 56);
- Government grants to smaller firms for consultancy on developing a community investment policy (pp 56-57);
- development of more management training in corporate social responsibility in business schools nationwide, in the wake of initiatives in this area by Manchester Business School (pp 58-59);
- action by committed businesses to encourage more suppliers and customers to become involved in community investment (pp 59-60);
- more development of management skills in the voluntary sector to facilitate links with business (pp 64-65);
- improved information exchange and coordination of initiatives between agencies at national level, perhaps in a regular Community Investment Forum (pp 67-69);
- the development of city-wide Community Investment Fora to provide a focus at the local level for information exchange, coordination of initiatives, development of partnerships, promotion of company involvement and strategic debate on local issues. A Community Investment Forum would be located in an appropriate existing organisation, such as a TEC or Chamber of Commerce or local authority, and would involve regular discussion between representatives of relevant local bodies from all sectors (pp 70-74).

5.   Case studies from three British cities

5.1 Birmingham has seen the development of a number of striking partnership ventures for urban renewal involving the private sector. Among the initiatives widely viewed as innovative and useful are:

- the Business Action Team (BAT), a partnership focussing on assistance for small firms in danger of going out of business (p 91);
- the Ten Company Group Equal Opportunity Project, a venture involving many companies in development of projects and policies designed to improve recruitment opportunities for people from ethnic minority communities (pp 92-93);
- Birmingham Heartlands, a major urban regeneration partnership between the Chamber of Commerce, the City Council and development companies (pp 93-97).

5.2 Bristol provides many examples of activity in the community by individual companies; the small firm Mosaic stands out as an example of commitment to a coherent, company-wide policy on community investment, and as an indication of how small companies can make an effective contribution (pp 130-133). Partnership ventures include the Bristol Initiative, a business-led strategic forum bringing together representatives of private, public and voluntary sector bodies in the city (pp 133-135).

5.3 Manchester has some of the most severe inner city problems in the UK, but has also seen a remarkable amount of urban renewal work in recent years and advances in the establishment of partnerships between business and the public and voluntary sectors. There has been a striking development of effective partnership between companies, public agencies and community groups to promote job opportunities and community regeneration in the inner city areas of Moss Side and Hulme. Leading firms have come together in a Business Support Group to work with public agencies and the local community, and this is widely regarded as a very promising development for the locality (pp 152-157).

Part I

Overview of Business Investment
in the Community

1 Introduction

1.1 Background to the study

In recent years there has been a considerable development of business investment in the community: financial contributions and other forms of support such as secondments, training and free provision of expertise, goods and services by companies to community initiatives and voluntary bodies. Donations and other types of contribution to the voluntary sector, community initiatives and the arts have increased substantially, and there has been a sustained effort by government and intermediary bodies such as Business in the Community (BitC) to recruit companies into the 'culture' of corporate giving and community involvement. Since the mid 1980s there has been a shift in emphasis in promotion of community action by business, away from the notion of 'charitable giving' and towards a focus on 'community investment' by companies, placing policies for community support in the mainstream of corporate activity.

The scale and nature of company activity in the community and the many issues of corporate and public policy it raises, are increasingly subjects of interest for managers in the private, public and voluntary sectors, social researchers and policy makers. This report is part of a growing body of work on business involvement in the community (see the bibliography in Appendix 4).

The report examines the reasons behind company action in the community, the benefits which community investment can bring to business, the organisational issues raised by community investment, and the obstacles to further development of the field in the UK and wider diffusion of good practices among firms.

The findings and recommendations reported here are directed to decision makers in business, whether or not their companies are already involved in supporting voluntary bodies, community initiatives and urban renewal projects; to practitioners in the voluntary and public sector who receive support from business or wish to develop links with companies; and to policy makers in government and intermediary bodies seeking to promote more business involvement in the community.

1.2 Aims of the research
The research project on which this report is based was initiated in June 1990 by the Department of the Environment's Inner Cities Directorate and the Policy Studies Institute. The aims of the research were:
• to examine the motivation behind companies' policies on community involvement and the ways in which those policies are developed and implemented, with particular reference to activities in areas with 'inner city' problems;
• to identify examples of 'good practice' in a variety of areas of activity by companies committed to involvement in the community;
• to identify organisational and external obstacles to adoption of good practice strategies by companies and suggest ways in which these might be overcome.

1.3 Research method
The research design chosen for the study involved case studies of three cities: Birmingham, Bristol and Manchester. Particular attention was paid to inner city areas in each centre in which the Government's City Action Teams and Task Forces are active, although the research work extended beyond these localities. The aim was to build up a picture of business involvement in community initiatives and urban renewal across the whole city, and to identify examples of good practice in individual firms' activities and in the operation of partnership ventures involving the private sector.

Each case study comprised interviews with key informants in the private sector, intermediary bodies and recipients of private sector support. In each city some twenty organisations were contacted for interview. The selection of businesses, intermediary bodies and community bodies for interview was based on two sources of information:

- initial interviews with City Action Teams and/or Task Force staff, who advised on key contacts in the private, public and voluntary sectors in their specific localities and in the wider city;
- further contacts offered by informants in the case study interviews.

For each case study, our aim was to contact 10-12 companies identified as potential examples of corporate good practice in community investment. We made efforts to obtain contacts with small and medium-sized enterprises in each locality as well as with the large firms which are prominent in community investment in each of the cities studied. In addition, we interviewed other actors in the city economy and community for their views on the role of the private sector and corporate good practice: for instance, Chambers of Commerce, community trusts, enterprise agencies, voluntary sector agencies and local authority representatives. Where appropriate, the local level interviews were supplemented by meetings with informants at national level. The range of issues which we sought to cover in the case studies is set out below.

Topics covered in interviews with companies
- value and direction of company investment in the community
- type of involvement and motivation
- development of company policies and procedures for allocating resources to community causes; how policies are implemented and assessed
- awareness of information sources; influences on company policy; use of intermediary agencies and other partners
- constraints on action in the community by the company

Topics covered in interviews with recipients of private sector support
- type of support received from private sector in the locality
- development of private sector support over recent years
- approaches to the private sector; arguments used to obtain support; use made of local networks and intermediary bodies
- obstacles to greater company involvement, ways of overcoming them

3

- flows of information; problems of awareness, coordination, communication, marketing; development of networks, follow-up communications to firms giving support
- ideas on what constitutes good practice among companies

Topics covered in interviews with business umbrella bodies, intermediary agencies

- development of activity in the locality; aims and methods, what successes and problems so far; what plans for future activity
- local networks linking companies, voluntary bodies and public agencies, and how companies get drawn into these networks
- the policies developed in relation to private sector involvement in the community
- arguments used in persuading companies to get involved
- obstacles to getting companies interested; reasons of companies which do not respond; problems of coordination
- ideas on good practice among firms; ideas on how to promote it.

It is important to note the limitations inherent in a qualitative study of this kind. The sample of companies cannot be claimed to be representative in any rigorous sense, and is biased deliberately towards organisations considered to be potential examples of corporate good practice in different community activities. Moreover, the whole field of research into company involvement in the community is affected at present by a number of difficulties posed by the nature of the subject:

- the inadequacies of published statistics on companies' support for charities and community initiatives (see section 2.2);
- the lack of a substantial base of research into company involvement in the UK;
- the fact that company investment in the community is a relatively new development for many firms, even for some of the largest corporate donors and sponsors;
- the fact that many of the initiatives aimed at bringing businesses into urban renewal and community investment are also relatively new and therefore cannot be rigorously assessed as yet;
- the unquantifiable nature of many of the benefits claimed for company investment in the community;
- the lack of monitoring and evaluation procedures among many companies involved in community activities (see section 3.2),

which make it difficult to assess even those benefits which may be quantifiable.

Nonetheless, despite these drawbacks and the inevitable reliance in a study of this size and scope on qualitative methods, principally key informant interviews, clear and valuable messages emerge from the research. It is important to stress that the findings reported below on the pattern of company policies and practices are supported by those obtained in Fogarty and Christie (1991) and by other recent studies such as Ernst and Young (1990), Metcalf, Pearson and Martin (1990), and Action Resource Centre (1989). The messages arising from the research are backed up by other recent work and in discussion with key informants in bodies promoting business action in the community. Although circumstances differ widely in the three cities visited, and among other cities in the UK, there are many problems common to them, and examples of good practice in tackling them may well be replicable in other cities and towns throughout the country.

1.4 Structure of the report

The rest of Part I consists of an analysis of the issues and messages arising from the city case studies reported in Part II, from our interviews with informants in organisations at national level, and from other recent research into company action in the community.

Chapter 2 defines the scope of community investment by business, examines the development of corporate activity over recent years, and looks at the reasons behind it and how companies are deriving various benefits from their involvement.

Chapter 3 considers the organisational issues for companies acting on their own on in concert with other businesses and organisations from the public and voluntary sector, and identifies examples of good practice.

Obstacles to the development of good practice are examined in Chapter 4, and recommendations are put forward for overcoming them, based on the examples of successful or promising action identified in the city case studies and in other recent research.

Finally in Part I, Chapter 5 summarises the key messages emerging from the research for businesses, intermediary bodies, public sector bodies and the voluntary sector.

Part II presents the three city case studies. For each city there is an overview of recent developments in the local economy and areas of urban renewal, followed by an examination of the key actors and networks involved in community regeneration and in bringing private sector support to initiatives. The discussion of company practice includes case studies of selected companies and initiatives which offer examples of good practice.

Part III provides basic reference material in four appendices. Appendix 1 presents a short guide for companies on developing a corporate policy on investment in the community. We hope that this set of guidelines will be of use to companies considering becoming involved in support for community initiatives or improving their current policies for community investment.

Appendices 2 and 3 give a list of organisations that can provide active and information to companies wishing to develop community links. Finally, Appendix 4 provides a select bibliography.

Key messages from the research, together with comprehensive information on organisations to contact and guidelines for corporate policy, have been published in a separate booklet, *Profitable Partnerships: an action guide for company investment in the community* (Christie, 1991), aimed at senior managers in business.

2 Getting Involved:
Reasons for Business Investment
in the Community

This section first of all defines the scope of business investment in the community and looks at how activity has developed over recent years. It then examines the reasons why companies get involved and how the various forms of business support for the community can be of benefit not just to the recipients but also to the companies involved.

2.1 The scope of business action in the community

'Community investment' by businesses embraces many types of activity, ranging from traditional forms of support for charitable bodies to action carried out through companies' mainstream commercial activities. In the research reported here we adopted a broad definition of community investment. The areas of activity we include in this definition, and which are found in all of the cities visited for the case studies reported in Part II, are described below.

- *Cash support* for voluntary organisations, enterprise agencies and for initiatives involving partnership between different sectors engaged in community renewal and economic regeneration in cities or regions (such as Business Leadership Teams, established under the auspices of Business in the Community). Cash support may take the form of one-off donations, regular donations, project funding, loans, matching grants (equalling monies raised by other parties for a specific cause), running a payroll giving scheme for employee involvement, or grants to intermediary bodies such as Community Trusts for distribution to voluntary groups.

- *Sponsorship* of projects or events: the area in which this has developed most strongly in recent years is business sponsorship of the arts, but sponsorship of environmental projects is becoming more important (see Forrester, 1990). *Social sponsorship* of community projects is promoted by bodies such as Action Match (see Appendix 2). Joint promotions, involving partnership between a company and a voluntary body, are another form of sponsorship: a recent development in this area is the emergence of 'affinity cards', credit card arrangements between voluntary bodies and companies through which the former receive a small donation for each transaction using the card.

- *Donation of equipment, products and materials*: giving in kind allows companies to pass on unwanted equipment such as office furniture to voluntary bodies and community groups; donate products for use or for raffle by the recipients; and donate office materials. Companies may also allow free use of facilities (rooms, offices, conference facilities) to community bodies.

- *Provision of staff time and expertise*: this type of support includes the *secondment* of staff either full-time or part-time for a set period; *provision of specialist advice* to community bodies on a one-off basis; involvement of staff on the boards of voluntary bodies, Enterprise Agencies, schools and other bodies such as Training and Enterprise Councils (TECs) and Business Leadership Teams; and employee volunteering of time and labour to community groups, either in their own time or in the company's time.

- *Recruitment and training*: companies can engage in *targeted recruitment measures* aimed at providing opportunities for specific groups such as the long-term unemployed, disabled people and ethnic minorities. Initiatives in this category include customised training and job interview guarantee (JIG) schemes designed to equip unemployed people for work in specific companies or with skills in particular demand among local employers.

- *Education-business partnerships*: companies can form links with schools and colleges and provide work experience for school students, operate COMPACT schemes and offer facilities for school visits, teacher placements, etc.

- *Local purchasing and sub-contracting*: companies can contribute to the local community through reviewing purchasing policy and placing orders and developing links with local firms, especially small enterprises.

- *Local investment measures*: companies can make a major difference to the economic and social well-being of the local community by reviewing investment decisions with community interests in mind, in order to maximise benefits to the local community and economy and minimise environmental disturbance. Measures may include investment in affordable housing schemes, property development for local small businesses, environmental improvements to local buildings and land, location of premises in an inner city area, and participation in urban renewal initiatives.

Clearly there is a very broad spread of activities here: the common factor is a decision by a company to direct resources into an activity with the aim of providing benefit to a community outside its own constituencies (employees, shareholders). An equally broad range of motivations may come into play as companies consider how to get involved in the local community. The 'traditional' forms of support – charitable donations and gifts in kind – tend to be associated with philanthropic motivation. The recipient benefits from the support, while the giver secures goodwill and, as one respondent put it, a 'warm glow', but does not seek to derive any more tangible benefits from the action. However, in the other areas listed above, the balance of benefits may be more even. Usually the principal aim will be to support a community body or cause or event, but the activity may produce indirect and sometimes direct benefits for the company. In the last four areas listed above – recruitment and training, education-business links, local purchasing, and local investment – the activities concerned are in the mainstream of company operations, and while the balance of motivation and benefits will be tilted towards the community, there may well be gains for the company which ultimately result in commercial benefit.

Before looking more closely at the motivation behind companies' involvement and the benefits they, as well as community groups, can derive from it, we need to consider the development of company activity in recent years and the rising importance of forms of support which go beyond 'charitable giving' and justify the use of the term 'community investment'.

2.2 The growth of business investment in the community
The current level of company expenditure on the community
Statistics on the scale of company support for charities and the wider community are published by the Charities Aid Foundation and the Directory of Social Change. The figures depend on the comprehensiveness of company reporting of their community activities, and there are many problems with this. The main difficulty is in estimating the value of non-cash support – secondments, other provision of staff time, use of facilities, giving in kind, and so on. Many companies, large and small, make no attempt to estimate the value of such community activities, and so reported figures in company accounts may often be well below the true level.

A recent estimate of the total value of community support by companies is shown below; it must be borne in mind that it certainly under-estimates total contributions by a considerable margin, especially for non-cash support such as secondments. It also excludes funds raised through school-business links and activity by employees in their own right with the encouragement of their firms – such as volunteering.

Estimated total community contributions by business, 1989

	£m	
Charitable donations	175	
Sponsorship	50	
Enterprise agencies	15	
Non-commercial advertising	20	
Joint promotions	15	
Secondments	25	
Total contributions	**300**	plus the value of gifts in kind

Source: Directory of Social Change, *Guide to Company Giving*, 1991.

The above figures conceal very wide variations in the practice of different companies, with high levels of expenditure by the top 50 corporate contributors in terms of percentage of pre-tax profits and amount spent per employee; and markedly lower rates from the rest of the top 400 contributors.

For all the flaws in the available data on the extent of company support, there is no doubt that it is substantial and has been growing in recent years. Declared charitable donations by the top 200 corporate donors doubled in real terms from 1987 to 1988. Measured in terms of donations per head of workforce, contributions by the top 200 givers almost trebled in real terms from 1977 to 1986. As for the percentage of pre-tax profits donated by the top 200, there has been only a slight increase in the 1980s, to just over 0.2 per cent on average as opposed to 0.17 per cent in 1977/8, but the substantial real rise in profits in recent years has meant that absolute contributions from this group have risen.

We return to the subject of statistics and levels of support in Chapters 3 and 4 below. Readers are referred to Fogarty and Christie (1991) for a full discussion of the available data on company contributions to charities and the community. Another measure of the rising importance of company involvement in the community in the UK is the amount of promotional activity designed to encourage and foster it.

Promotion of company involvement in recent years
It was not until the early 1980s that community investment by business began to move up the agenda of voluntary agencies and promotional bodies, but there are now numerous agencies promoting business involvement in the community: details of some of the leading agencies which can assist companies in developing their activities are given in Appendix 3.

Several factors have contributed to the rise in awareness and public promotion of the role of companies in the community.
• The growth of unemployment, especially youth unemployment, in the late 1970s, and growing concern in the 1970s over the disadvantages of ethnic minorities in the labour market, led to the establishment of bodies such as *Fullemploy Group* for the promotion of new employment and enterprise.

- Changes in the political climate after the election of the Conservative Government in 1979:
  - funding constraints on local authority social services and an increased emphasis on the role of the voluntary sector in the provision of services;
  - the promotion of 'active citizenship' by individuals and companies and policies aimed at increasing the role of private and voluntary sector bodies in education, training, the arts, urban regeneration and the environment;
  - substantial growth in the number and range of community initiatives on enterprise, training and job creation which demand an expanded role for the voluntary sector and for business in the management of projects.

- A growing sense among business leaders in the 1970s that private enterprise had an unfavourable image in many areas, and that a more positive picture of the role of business needed to be conveyed to communities in the inner cities, to schools and colleges, and to the public generally.

- Alarm among business leaders over the threat of alienation of whole sections of the population in disadvantaged areas from mainstream economic and social life, and of consequent social unrest and urban decay as experienced in many American cities. The riots of the 1980s in cities such as Bristol and Liverpool were a major stimulus to action for a number of large companies in the UK.

- The example set by American businesses from the late 1970s onwards in spending on charitable giving, employee volunteering and other forms of community involvement. The volume of corporate giving expanded and many initiatives for promotion of more company involvement took off. By the late 1980s charitable contributions by US corporations were averaging 1.8 per cent of pre-tax profits (see Fogarty and Christie, 1991, chapter 6).

- The involvement of many companies in the 1980s in schemes intended to limit the damage done to communities by industrial restructuring and large-scale redundancy programmes.

One effect of the combined force of all of these pressures has been the development of many new forms of promotional activity aimed at raising company awareness of the scope for business action. In 1981

Business in the Community (BitC) was established as a partnership of major companies for the promotion of greater involvement by business in local economic development and community regeneration. BitC now has some 450 member organisations, including public and voluntary sector bodies, and growth in membership has been steady throughout the last ten years. BitC promotes and oversees Enterprise Agencies throughout the country, and has developed initiatives in areas such as local purchasing and environmental regeneration through its numerous 'Target Teams'. BitC has also overseen the development of new forms of partnership and promotion of business activity in the community, for example:

- The Per Cent Club, an association of companies which have made a commitment to devoting at least half of one per cent of pre-tax profits to supporting community activities, whether via donations, staff time, or any of the other methods listed in section 2.1 above. In 1990 the Per Cent Club decided to raise the guideline percentage to one per cent of pre-tax profits by 1992. Local clubs have been set up in Newcastle and Sheffield
- Business Leadership Teams (BLTs), partnerships of leading business people and key personnel form the public and voluntary sectors in particular localities, which act as a forum for the promotion of initiatives for economic and community regeneration. BLTs have been set up in areas such as Blackburn, Bristol, the North West and Sheffield.

Business activity is also promoted and supported by a wide range of more specialised agencies and initiatives which have grown up since the 1970s. For example:

- Action Resource Centre, which promotes secondments of various kinds by business;
- Action Match, which promotes the development of social sponsorship by companies;
- The Association for Business Sponsorship of the Arts (ABSA), which represents business sponsors and promotes and facilitates sponsorship;
- Common Purpose, a new initiative based on an American model, is now becoming widely established throughout the UK after being piloted in Newcastle and Coventry. It aims to provide training in community leadership to senior people from all sectors of particular communities. The training brings together key decision

makers from different walks of life in order that they can exchange ideas and experience and form new networks of collaboration and information exchange;

- The Groundwork Foundation, which works in partnership with many companies on projects for environmental improvement in and around urban areas.

There are many other voluntary agencies which work with and receive support from business in promoting enterprise creation, training schemes, small business support and so on. Their promotional activity in recent years has been supplemented by initiatives from government aimed at stimulating the private sector into increased community activity. For example:

- improved tax incentives for individual and corporate giving to charitable bodies, and also to enterprise agencies and Training and Enterprise Councils (TECs);
- the introduction of the TECs in England and Wales and of Local Enterprise Companies (LECs) in Scotland. The complete network will consist of 82 TECs and 22 LECs, responsible for delivery of training and enterprise support programmes in their localities. Two-thirds of TEC boards must be private sector employers at chief executive level. The TECs bring business leaders together with representatives from all sectors of the local community – public agencies, trade unions, education, local government and the voluntary sector. The TECs also have resources for the development of education-business partnership schemes, and have been assigned a wider role in the promotion of community economic regeneration beyond their remit for management of training and enterprise programmes, and thus form a new mechanism for community investment by business;
- the development of many central government schemes for urban renewal, designed to stimulate private sector investment in property development and environmental regeneration in the cities. The many initiatives launched by different government departments are grouped under the umbrella of the 'Action for Cities' programme, coordinated by the Department of the Environment (see Appendix 3). Among the main initiatives to emerge in recent years are:
  - the Urban Programme, a mechanism designed to help local authorities in inner city areas tackle economic, environmental

and social problems. Priorities include projects intended to improve the employment prospects of inner city residents;

- Urban Development Corporations, the main mechanism for using public funds to 'pump-prime' private sector investment in derelict inner city areas;
- City Grant, introduced to encourage and assist development in the inner cities by attracting private sector investment. The Grant is intended to bridge the gap between development cost and values on completion, enabling the developer to make a reasonable return;
- City Action Teams (CATs) and Task Forces, which seek to improve the coordination and targeting of existing government programmes, and develop innovative approaches to the economic regeneration of particular inner city areas;
- training and enterprise initiatives, chiefly aimed at helping unemployed people back into work and supporting small firms and enterprise agencies; these programmes are being taken over by the new TECs and LECs.

There is, then, a plethora of recent schemes and initiatives designed to involve the private sector in community action in general, encompassing charitable giving and forms of support which come closer to mainstream business activities – in training, property development, land reclamation, and so on. Among the leading promotional bodies there is a consensus that it is not enough simply to promote *charitable* giving by firms, important thought it is to both companies and communities. They place increasing emphasis, as do government initiatives, on the promotion of forms of support which potentially can help the company achieve business objectives as well as contribute to community renewal. In short, there is now a widespread move towards appealing to companies' sense of *enlightened self-interest* as well as to their sense of *social responsibility*. Business is being encouraged to think of 'community investment' (the phrase favoured by one of the biggest corporate donors, IBM (UK) Limited) rather than simply of 'charitable giving'.

One of the main factors behind this shift in emphasis has been the recognition of the threats and opportunities presented by the decline of many inner city areas over recent decades and the sharp downturn in many cities' fortunes in the late 1970s and early 1980s. The next section considers the special impact of urban problems on the whole field of business involvement in the community.

Business and the cities
The recessions of the 1970s and the sharp decline in manufacturing employment in the UK especially in the period 1980-2, placed a heavy burden on the cities. Already deprived areas were badly affected by job loss, the collapse of local businesses and loss of population. Over the years many localities, whether truly in the 'inner city' or in marginal outer suburbs, had entered a downward spiral, with the loss of businesses, unemployment, crime, dependency on welfare, poor housing and infrastructure, and racial discrimination all reinforcing each other. Particular localities, given the often inaccurate general label 'inner cities', have become concentrations of severe social problems: communities with reduced capacity for self-regeneration, in which many citizens feel they have no 'stake' in society, and plagued by persistent high levels of long-term unemployment, crime, drug abuse, and discrimination.

The recession of the early 1980s, the riots of 1980 and 1981 in Bristol and Liverpool and elsewhere, and the Birmingham riots of the mid 1980s all played a part in alerting business leaders to the need for action, following a long period of withdrawal by many firms from inner city areas. Another important factor was the example, in two ways, of the experience of the United States. First, there was from the late 1970s an upsurge in corporate giving in the USA and in business involvement in urban renewal. Many British business leaders returned from study visits to America impressed by the renewal of 'inner city' areas in cities such as Baltimore and Boston. Second, many of them also returned with a sense of horror at what they had seen of the decay of neighbourhoods in cities such as Chicago, and the seemingly hopeless position of the citizens there, who had come to constitute an urban 'underclass', economically marginalised and completely alienated from mainstream society. As the CBI Task Force on Business and Urban Regeneration put it in its report *Initiatives Beyond Charity* (CBI, 1988, p.19):

> The most deprived parts of some North American cities stand as a chilling example of what could be in store for us. Lawndale, on the south side of Chicago, represents a future to be avoided at almost any cost.

The scale of the problems, and the importance to the private sector of the overall economic and social health of Britain's cities, was a key factor behind the establishment of Business in the Community in 1981, and of the CBI's Task Force on urban renewal, which was set up in 1987 and reported its recommendations on business action in the inner cities the following year. As the chairman of the Task Force noted in the report cited above,

> Business has a massive stake in the nation's cities. Employees and customers live in them; many companies operate from city locations, and their balance sheets reflect the cost and value of the assets involved; the retail, banking, insurance, tourism, leisure, manufacturing and construction industries will all be affected by the economic vitality and social health of the communities concerned (CBI, 1988, p.7).

The report of the CBI Task Force, and publications by BitC on inner cities, reflect the shift in the debate on corporate support for the community towards an emphasis on enlightened self-interest. While an appeal is still made to the business leader's sense of moral concern and social responsibility, it is stressed that the nature of inner city problems is such that charitable giving, even at a much higher level than at present, is on its own inadequate to the task in hand. There is a need not just for more 'philanthropic' support but also for the injection of resources which can only come from major commercial investment decisions.

This perspective means a new focus on the potential benefits to business as well as to the community from putting large-scale resources into urban regeneration. In terms of business opportunities, depressed local economies mean reduced markets for companies' products and services; unemployed and under-qualified citizens mean a waste of potentially skilled employees; the creation of ghetto areas and an underclass means the risk of social explosions which will damage the business community among others; derelict land means a waste of potential building sites for housing, offices, factories and parks, whose creation would generate wealth and opportunities for employment and new enterprises.

Less tangibly, it is argued that involvement can benefit businesses by allowing new opportunities for training and career development, improving staff relations, creating new links with local suppliers and customers, improving the image of business in general and committed firms in particular, with the potential for positive effects on recruitment and orders as a result.

Ways in which business can get involved in the renewal of the cities are set out in detail in the CBI Task Force report. The model of activity is based on the establishment to enable business leaders, in partnership with other sectors, to create major projects for urban renewal which will generate wealth, stimulate new enterprise and job creation, and build up local confidence. Successful regeneration projects would attract more investment into an area, and a 'virtuous circle' would be created.

The process of revival as set out in *Initiatives Beyond Charity* and in BitC publications has three key elements, vital to its success:

- the need for business commitment to community investment to be *long-term*: quick commercial returns are unlikely to be compatible with regeneration which benefits the whole community, and large scale urban renewal is a matter of years, if not decades, as the American experience shows;
- the need for a *multi-faceted* approach to renewal: the problems of the inner city are multifarious and interlocking, and a simple property-led approach is liable to leave many social problems untouched;
- this leads to the recognition of the need for a *partnership* approach between business, local and central government agencies and community bodies. If the resources required are 'beyond charity', they are also far beyond the means of companies acting alone. Hence the need, as recognised by government, for the large scale injection of public funds into renewal in order to attract business investment. Moreover, the need for a multi-faceted approach in turn demands the collaboration of bodies with many different skills at different levels, from strategic planning down to the grassroots, and the mix of expertise required cannot be located in any one organisation or sector.

The problems of the cities, then, have been especially important in the development of company involvement in the community. They have played a key role in the growth of interest in action which can benefit firms as well as communities, and led to the development of ideas about business action in partnership with public bodies and community groups which go beyond traditional charitable links. And since the inner cities have many problems common to other areas, but in a particular concentrated and intractable form, it may be that approaches which work or show promise there will have wider application in other cities and towns.

However, before we look at how companies are getting involved in regenerating city communities, we need to examine in more detail the reasons why companies have taken action and what benefits they, as well as the community, feel they are gaining from it.

2.4 Social responsibility and enlightened self-interest
The importance of social responsibility

There is no doubt that, of late, promotional agencies and government bodies have based their appeal to business to get more involved in community action largely on the notion of enlightened self-interest. Informants in promotional agencies say that they detect a growing emphasis among companies, especially the larger corporate donors, on activity which provides benefit both to the community recipient and to the firm; and that, increasingly, voluntary bodies and intermediary agencies are dealing with the private sector on a business basis – providing a service in exchange for financial or other support.

The move towards enlightened self-interest has important implications, which we will examine below, but it needs to be borne in mind that the change in emphasis does *not* mean that promotional bodies or companies are downgrading the role of a sense of corporate social responsibility, or 'altruism', or 'philanthropy'. The desire to be a good corporate citizen, and disinterested support for charitable causes, remain powerful motivating factors behind company involvement. This is clear from our case study research and from other recent research work.

Fogarty and Christie (1991) report the results of a postal survey of medium-sized companies (500-2999 employees) involved in charitable support in the UK. Asked about the relative importance of different motivations and influences on their policy towards company giving, nearly 60 per cent of respondents rated 'social responsibility' as very important, while 12 per cent gave the same rating to 'enlightened self interest' – less than the proportion citing 'views of chairman or managing director' as a significant influence. Moreover, one quarter of respondents claimed that 'enlightened self interest' was not important as a motivating factor for them. A small survey of companies involved in secondment, carried out by Action Resource

Centre (Action Resource Centre, 1989), found that respondents most commonly cited 'Making a contribution to the community' as their main objective in providing secondees, ahead of various benefits to the company.

Our case study work confirms that for many companies the desire to 'put something back into the community', regardless of any self-interest, is a strong motivating force. This is the case among companies of very different sizes and areas of activity. Hewlett Packard's 'Corporate Objectives' discuss involvement in the community in terms of good citizenship, which means 'identifying our interests with those of the community'. In Manchester, Clayton Aniline's company brochure states that '...business is not an end in itself and that it must serve people and society'. In Bristol, the small consultancy firm Mosaic offers a striking example of company-wide commitment to social responsibility. There are many examples of companies in which the family tradition of the owners, or loyalty to a particular locality built up over a long period, or the influence of particular individuals, leads to a strong commitment to corporate philanthropy.

Social responsibility and corporate self-interest as a continuum
It is important to emphasise the role of social responsibility in companies' outlook on community involvement, since the recent move towards promotion of enlightened self-interest can sometimes give the impression that altruism and philanthropy are in some way less valuable as motives, or that they are even opposed to the development of policies based more on self-interest. In fact, of course, there is no clear dividing line at all between 'social responsibility' and 'enlightened self-interest'.

This is evident from recent research and from our case studies. Many, if not most companies, have a range of activities aimed at supporting the wider community, and a range of motivations, rather than a single one, come into play. Firms typically distinguish sharply in terms of organisation, budgets and motivation between activities such as sponsorship, in which the balance is tilted towards commercial benefits and public relations, and charitable donations, which may be given via a company trust, a community trust, or even anonymously. However, in many areas of community action by firms, the balance is much more even, and a mixture of motivating factors comes into play.

For example, school-business links involve a degree of altruism and also an element of self-interest in relation to company image and recruitment; many forms of charitable support may involve some long-term considerations of benefit to company image in the community, or of the overall image of business; companies carrying out secondment policies increasingly are encouraged to think not just of the benefits to the recipient body but also of the potential for benefits to the firm from secondees' exposure to new demands on their management skills.

So the key point to be made about social responsibility and enlightened self-interest is that they form a *continuum* of motivating factors for business investment in the community. They cannot be neatly disentangled, and altruistic motivation is certainly not to be regarded as 'inferior' or antithetical to policies involving recognition of business benefits from community support. This is underlined by respondents in companies visited for this and other studies. At Kellogg in Manchester, managers responsible for the company's community policies stress that their activities are spread along the whole spectrum from concern for good corporate citizenship to self-interest. Barclays Bank underlines the intimate links between social responsibility and overall business interests:

> ...as we make profit *in* the community, it is right that we should make efforts *for* the community. It is, in a sense, enlightened self-interest; people are more likely to bank with us if we are known to have a social conscience (John Quinton, Chairman, in *Barclays Briefing*, no.75, February 1988).

Another point needs to be made clearly about the balance between motivations. A number of respondents stressed that the nature of the influence behind company action in the community was not as important as the honesty and commitment brought to bear in dealings with recipients. As Kellogg's Corporate Affairs Manager put it:

> Anywhere along the spectrum from altruism to self-interest is legitimate as long as the company is aware and honest about its motives. Communities will respect any honestly expressed motivation.

The special role of enlightened self-interest
What factors have led to the recent emphasis on enlightened self-interest? As described in the previous section, the nature of the

problems of the cities provides some of the answers. The resources required cannot be tapped via charitable policies in the private sector: many problems can only be tackled by treating them in part as investment opportunities.

Another key element is the recognition that measures for urban renewal and community regeneration need to strengthen communities' sense of confidence and self-respect. There are particular problems here for any approach based on a charitable 'gift relationship', in which a donor gives to a passive recipient. At worst, in some areas 'charity' can be resented as patronising, especially if the support is 'one-off' and handed out by an organisation with no stake in the community. As one of our respondents, a director of an Enterprise Agency in an inner city area put it, initial support from the private sector for his venture was 'altruism to help some poor people'. As dialogue went on with the private sector, business leaders came to realise that they were needed to provide a mechanism for economic regeneration via self-employment in the locality. This called for a long-term, hands-on commitment to partnership with community groups, and deployment of the firms' mainstream business expertise rather than charitable funds. Other respondents argued that in many areas of community action the recipients of company support preferred to be involved in a commercial exercise which had 'mainstream' backing from the company. For instance, one provider of training schemes for the long-term unemployed argued that the last thing that people in this category wanted was to receive 'philanthropic' support; his approach was '100 per cent commercial':

> The long-term unemployed like that because they know we're not doing them any favours.

A further reason for the promotion of enlightened self-interest is the need to recruit many more companies into the 'culture' of community involvement. The scene is dominated by major companies such as Marks & Spencer, IBM, Allied Dunbar and British Telecom, with large and sophisticated community investment programmes and policies, based on a mix of charitable giving and other activities. Despite the rise in company expenditure reported in section 2.2 above, there is huge scope for much more activity by existing corporate donors and for many more firms to get involved. Promotional bodies and many respondents in companies feel that the key to activating more firms, especially small and medium-sized companies, is to emphasise that involvement can bring benefit to the firm as well as to the community. Given the range of demands upon company purses and staff time in an increasingly competitive environment, it is in the interests of companies and voluntary and community bodies alike to look 'beyond charity' towards more businesslike relationships which are potentially *mutually* beneficial. While many potential benefits to the company may be hard, if not impossible, to measure, business does indeed stand to gain in various ways from getting involved. What examples emerge from our research findings and those of other recent studies?

The range of benefits to companies from community investment

It is useful, in considering the range of benefits which can be gained by companies from community investment, to distinguish between *long-term* benefits associated with *strategic enlightened self-interest*, and those which are more short-term, associated with a *tactical* approach. As with social responsibility and self-interest, these need to be seen as part of a continuum rather than easily distinguishable elements of company activity. And of course, company policies may include both strategic and tactical elements.

Long-term strategic benefits from community involvement

At the strategic, long-term end of the spectrum, benefits identified by companies in our case study cities included the following.

- Long-term revival of economic activity in disadvantaged areas was often cited by respondents: helping communities and investing in the local economy would eventually bring new custom and business opportunities as overall local prosperity spread. As a respondent put it, 'If people do not have disposable income they cannot buy our products'. Another referred to the chronic problem of bad debts in his company's area, which had a serious impact on the firm. If the company could help through its community policies to reduce local unemployment and improve the very poor quality housing stock, then related problems such as bad debts and high levels of crime might eventually be alleviated.
- The development of a potential pool of skilled employees in inner city localities was also frequently mentioned by respondents. Reinvigoration of the local labour market, to which company support for training, enterprise creation, targeting of employment

opportunities on groups suffering from discrimination, could help attract more business into the area and give the company an increased pool for local recruitment. As a respondent from a group of firms in Birmingham collaborating on equal opportunities initiatives said, this kind of strategy was simply good business sense – otherwise his firm and others would be missing out on 'mountains of talent in Birmingham's ethnic minority communities'.

• The maintenance and enhancement of company image and goodwill in the wider community was also frequently cited. This was sometimes very specifically related to a company's activities. For instance, Clayton Aniline, a Manchester chemicals firm, is by the nature of its potentially hazardous business especially concerned to maintain good will locally: the factory is situated next to a residential area in East Manchester and the company has a strategic objective of 'living in harmony' with the local community. A telling and unusual case of the potential of the long-term public relations effect has been provided by Shell UK, whose recent fine for pollution of the Mersey would, said the judge, have been far higher than the £1m imposed if he had not taken into account the company's track record in community support, arts sponsorship and environmental regeneration schemes.

• A related point is the contribution made by involvement in the community to a company's 'self-image' – the effect on employee motivation. A manager at Kellogg related his firm's overall approach in part to the need for a well-motivated workforce: working in a depressed area would lead to demotivation and loss of staff, and the need to avoid this was an added reason for seeking to invest in the local economy and community. The impact on company self-image and motivation was also important for a small 'values-driven' firm such as Mosaic in Bristol, whose ethos of community involvement by all employees is likely to be a major source of attraction to potential recruits. Schemes allowing staff time for community work and volunteering, as run by major firms such as Allied Dunbar, IBM and Grand Metropolitan, may have long-term benefits in retention of staff and overall motivation, and also bring new knowledge and skills into the organisation from employees' exposure to new activities and problems. The same is felt to be the case by companies involved in secondment programmes. The spin-off benefits for staff career development and acquisition of management skills are stressed by Action Resource Centre in its promotion of mid-career secondment and short-term 'development assignments' of staff to community bodies.

- Similarly, there are long range benefits from community investment in terms of the improved image a company can present to potential employees. This factor may be expected to increase in importance for firms seeking recruits, especially in the graduate market, as demographic change heightens competition for qualified people and as awareness of environmental issues grows. New graduates appear to be increasingly interested in the values of potential employers, especially in relation to environmental standards. The involvement, on a substantial scale, of many companies visited for this study in the development of their local TEC, also reflects a recognition of the strategic benefits for recruitment that can flow from involvement in broad community initiatives.

- A further factor is the long-term effect on company image among customers as well as employees and potential recruits. Companies such as Marks & Spencer and Body Shop seem to have improved their overall appeal to customers through their reputation for community investment (see Henley Centre, *Planning for Social Change*, 1989). This aspect of long-term benefit from community involvement can also be related to wider market considerations. IBM has related its environmental policies to its broad concern with being a company known for high quality in its products, processes, employee and customer relations. In Manchester, our respondent at Royal Mail related the company's activities in the community to its broad strategy for *total quality management* (TQM) – an emphasis on continuous quality improvement in all areas of the organisation's activities.

This is an area which deserves more exploration by companies, promotional agencies and researchers. As consumer pressures mount in relation to environmental standards, and increasing competition puts a premium on product and service quality, so there may be long-term value for companies in integrating their overall market strategies more closely with policies for community action and environmental protection, in the interest of maintaining a reputation among customers, employees and potential employees as high quality enterprises. Excellence in one area should imply excellence in another: companies that place a high value on providing a quality service to one of their internal and external 'communities' (employees, shareholders, customers, suppliers, local community, national community) should aim for consistency of quality in relation to all of them. Companies moving in this direction, such as IBM, Marks & Spencer and, at the other end of the size range, Mosaic, are obviously very much exceptions at present; but the pressures for change, and the long-term benefits that these firms feel that they gain, cannot be ignored by others.

More immediate benefits from community involvement

Action taken in response to long-term and strategic problems, such as recruitment difficulties related to demographic factors and lack of adequately skilled labour, can bring significant benefits to companies as well as to communities over the short term. Our case studies found several examples of companies which were reaping benefits in terms of improved recruitment and retention from involvement in programmes for pre-employment training and schemes aimed at disadvantaged groups. In a study devoted to this particular field of activity (Crowley-Bainton and White, 1990), PSI researchers identified considerable benefits to employers, notably those working in inner city areas, from their involvement in training and employing unemployed people. Their key conclusions are that:
- most types of organisation have scope to consider recruiting from the unemployed pool;
- recruits from the unemployed pool, suitably trained, can be supplied to a wide range of jobs;
- pre-recruitment training targeted at ethnic minority members or other special groups can bring new sources of high-quality talent into an organisation;
- recruitment initiatives can often produce spin-off benefits, for instance increased applications from ethnic minority groups, positive publicity for the firm, and improved community and customer relations.

Benefits claimed by firms operating in inner city areas included:
- unexpectedly high quality of potential recruits;

- favourable cost comparisons with other recruitment methods;
- improved community relations;
- discovery of a new and plentiful supply of potential recruits;
- improved retention rates.

Other tactical self-interest reasons for community involvement include the need to win local goodwill on moving into an area or seeking to develop new sites; and the benefits to be gained from operating as a trainer on publicly-funded schemes for training unemployed people. These motivations came together in the case of one company visited, which was required by the local authority to take on local recruits on redeveloping a site in an inner city area when expanding its production facilities. This has proved extremely successful for the company, which has reported many of the benefits listed above in taking on recruits from the unemployed pool and the ethnic minority groups in its locality. Another firm found that its involvement in the community, via the operation of public training schemes, was profitable as well as a means of equipping the long-term unemployed for the labour market.

The tactical motivation can therefore lead to substantial gains which are long-lasting in their effects. It is also one of the 'ways in' to a more strategic, proactive and long-term commitment to community involvement. This was the case in the two companies mentioned above. Our respondent in the firm running training schemes had taken up a place on one of the target teams of his local TEC; and the other company, as noted by a community leader, had moved from initial reluctance and short-term considerations to a much more positive and committed attitude towards community action – in fact, he observed, they were now even 'giving lectures' on the subject.

Motivation and implications for the organisation of community involvement

It should be clear from the foregoing discussion that our original idea of a continuum of motivation, ranging from philanthropic altruism to self-interest at the other, with varying degrees of mixed motives in between, needs to be made more complex. There is also a continuum of enlightened self-interest, from a strategic perspective at one end to a more tactical and commercial approach at the other. Different forms of community support are associated with different parts of the continuum, as illustrated in the diagram below.

Mainstream Business

eg - Recruitment
    - Training
    - Purchasing
	eg - Affinity Cards
	    - Environment
	    - Unit Trust

Self-interest ——————————————— **Social responsibility**

eg - Targeted Recruitment
    - Customised Training
    - Mid-career Secondments
    - Enterprise Agency Support
    - Marketing Sponsorship
    - Support for TECs/LECs
    - Local purchasing
	eg - Donations to Charity
	    - Sponsorship of
	      Community Activities
	    - Pre-retirement
	      Secondments

Community Involvement

Source: Robert Charleston, TSB Group

We need to consider one other reason for the recent shift in emphasis towards promotion of enlightened self-interest as a motive for corporate support for the community. This is the view that a perspective which incorporates potential benefits for the company as well as for the community has most chance of becoming fully integrated in a company's culture and mainstream decision-making processes; and that resources adequate to the tasks involved in inner city renewal will only be unlocked if companies treat community investment as part of their central business activities (training, personnel relations, purchasing, marketing) rather than as a marginal activity. In short, getting companies involved in long-term, mainstream commitment to the community and organised to support it calls for an appeal to enlightened self-interest as well as a sense of 'philanthropic' social responsibility. It demands that companies develop a more 'holistic' approach to involvement, building up activities in the different segments of the diagram above to form a broad portfolio of community investment policies which reach into the mainstream of the business.

In the next section we look how companies are getting involved in their local communities and what lessons their experience provides about good practice.

3 Getting Organised: Good Practice by Businesses in the Community

So far we have considered why companies are being urged to get involved in community support and what some of the benefits may be from an approach that includes elements of enlightened self-interest as well as of altruism and a sense of good citizenship. In this section we look in more detail at how companies get involved and organise their activities, and we attempt to highlight cases that illustrate good practice.

3.1 Defining good practice

First we need to consider what 'good practice' means in the context of community investment by business. Given the frequent lack of monitoring of projects and rigorous assessment of policies, and the inadequacies of much of the available statistical data about company involvement generally, it is essential to adopt a pragmatic view of good practice. We have looked for *examples of activity and organisation that are felt by the companies concerned to be successful or at least promising; that are seen as successful or promising by community bodies and other organisations in contact with companies; and that are potentially reproducible outside the area in question by other companies.*

Good practice is not only needed in companies' internal organisation but also in its external policies for links with the community. There are important issues for good practice in the creation of wider networks of activity: partnerships involving multi-firm links for community action; and partnerships bringing the private sector together with public sector agencies and the voluntary sector. Moreover, good practice within companies will only flourish if there is helpful practice in the wider environment for company action in the community – among public bodies, community groups and intermediary agencies.

In the following sub-sections we look first at the range of company activities; then at organisational issues for companies getting involved in community support; and finally at issues arising from the operation of networks and partnerships involving the private sector.

3.2   The range of company activity in the community

The city case studies revealed a wide range of types of involvement by companies, and the overall pattern which emerged was similar to that shown by other recent studies (see Ernst and Young, 1990; Fogarty and Christie, 1991).

Much the most common form of support was *traditional charitable giving*, whether in cash or kind; some respondents said that it was much easier to obtain donations in kind rather than in cash. Charitable giving was found across the whole spectrum of companies. Among larger firms, there was frequent support in cash or kind for enterprise agencies and small firm support initiatives, and for partnership initiatives such as TECs and Business Leadership Teams.

Amongst the larger firms there were often substantial budgets for *sponsorship*, whether in the arts, sport or national promotional campaigns. Environmental and social sponsorship initiatives were much less common overall, but several respondents saw these as growing fields for action by companies.

Secondment programmes were largely the preserve of major companies, and even among some of the big firms there were constraints on full-time secondments because of tight policies on headcount. However, there were numerous examples of short-term assignments, either on a full-time or part-time basis, which provided valuable expert advice and support to community groups and enterprise agencies. The example of the Business Action Team in Birmingham, which provides small firms at risk of bankruptcy with expertise, was a striking case of a form of support which deserves emulation in other cities. National Westminster's supply of business development managers to inner city initiatives in Birmingham is another example of a mechanism for secondment and provision of expertise. Community groups often stressed the importance of specialist advice and skill transfer by companies, which was frequently more significant to the success of community ventures than direct financial support. A key instance of this is the need for training and continuing support in order to allow community groups to make the most of donated equipment: in Manchester an enterprise agency received consultancy and management skills in information systems development from a corporate supporter. Donated or heavily discounted equipment, especially computers, can be of great benefit to community groups, but the input of training and expert advice adds enormous value and can ensure the success of the basic donation.

Provision of training opportunities for voluntary sector organisations is a potentially excellent form of community investment, making use of company expertise and transferring key skills to voluntary bodies, which are often in great need of better management and financial skills. An example of good practice in this area is the development by IBM of a 'Creative Mangagement Skills' course targeted at managers from the voluntary sector, and which was designed by an IBM employee who had previously been seconded to a charity. More widespread provision of their own management training expertise by other firms would be a highly effective form of community investment, and would be greatly welcomed by the voluntary sector – IBM's courses have been 'massively' over-subscribed.

A valuable form of support that was often encountered, especially in relation to large firms, was giving senior staff time to join the boards and management teams of community organisations or partnership bodies such as TECs, or to serve on hospital or school boards as governors. In Manchester the director of the enterprise agency AED in Moss Side and Hulme cited a case of this kind of support. The secondment of a bank manager from Barclays was felt to be a great success, and this was followed up by the manager joining the board of AED as a director; this was seen by the head of AED as excellent practice in company support. Clearly there are potential benefits in this sort of activity for companies as well as for recipient bodies: there is the possibility of influence on policy and the development of new contacts and knowledge of the community.

Employee volunteering schemes were found among the major companies, and in some cases, such as Grand Metropolitan, were regarded firmly as part of the mainstream of company activity and culture. The example of Mosaic in Bristol, which allocates a percentage of staff time to volunteering in the community, shows that this form of action is not necessarily confined to big firms. One respondent from a major company said that it was likely that his firm would eventually specify employee community involvement as a *contractual requirement* of employment.

Links of various kinds with schools were common, and in this area there was considerable scope for action by small and medium-sized firms as well as by major companies. Links took the form of work experience schemes, support for local Compact initiatives, donations of equipment such as computers, allocation of staff time to visit schools and sit on boards, and secondment arrangements. An example of the last mentioned activity came from Grand Metropolitan Community Services, which offers schoolteachers placements in the company and allocates employees time to change places and work in schools: our respondent emphasised that this scheme gave new insights and skills not just to the teachers but also to Grand Metropolitan staff.

Involvement in training initiatives and targeted recruitment schemes was an important part of community involvement in the cities for many firms, and again there was scope for action by small and medium-sized firms as well as large ones. Construction firms such as Wimpey and Jarvis were involved in support for training ventures in inner city areas in Bristol and Manchester respectively, and Jarvis regarded their involvement in training long-term unemployed people as an aspect of mainstream commercial practice, directly profitable to the firm as well as of benefit to the inner city community.

Examples of major commitment to support for training in the inner cities were provided by Grand Metropolitan Community Services and Rover Group in Birmingham, and by Scottish and Newcastle Breweries in Manchester among others. These are described in the city case studies in Part II.

Local recruitment, purchasing and investment policies may be pursued by companies without being regarded by them as part of their community support activities. All of these policies, however, can be framed within a wider strategy with benefit for the local economy and community in mind. For several firms local recruitment went hand in hand with support for training initiatives designed to equip local people for jobs: if suitable people were available on the doorstep, then naturally local recruitment would increase and more firms would be drawn into the area either to recruit or to invest. Manchester, in particular, provided a number of examples of good practice in local recruitment, among small and medium-sized firms as well as large employers such as Royal Mail Letters. This form of support is obviously a vital one to inner city communities in which above average levels of long-term unemployment and discrimination are found; as one Task Force leader stressed in enlarging on this point, 'The best private sector contribution is a job'.

Local purchasing schemes specifically intended to benefit local economies were not common, and several respondents said that this was an area in which initiatives were hard to organise. In particular, there was often a lack of systematic information on local suppliers, and one informant argued that registers of suppliers were essential as a basis for concerted local action by larger companies. British Telecom, which operates a major programme of different forms of support for inner city ventures, noted that in many areas of purchasing its requirements would simply overwhelm small local firms, and that purchasing schemes needed to be carefully designed and targeted on practicable levels of activity.

Local investment policies aimed at community support as well as commercial benefit range from the very large scale urban renewal projects to be found in all three of our case study cities and in other urban development areas of the UK to initiatives by individual firms. Major infrastructural ventures may help inner city communities in the long run by stimulating local economic activity in general; targeted action by companies in their investment decisions can help much more directly. The Birmingham case study in Chapter 7 provides two examples from firms at different ends of the size range: the small firm Bucknall Austin's decision to relocate to an inner city location rather than a green field site, and IMI's major initiative in developing derelict sites and linking this project to its local training activities. It is important for the confidence of inner city communities that companies invest in them and operate in them – the fact that companies are *there* counts for a great deal on its own. The point can be illustrated negatively by the dismay generated by decisions to pull out: for instance, by banks in areas such as Moss Side and Hulme in Manchester.

Several key messages emerge from this brief overview of activities, and are underlined in the city case studies.

- There are very many positive examples of company action in the community among companies in many different sectors and of many sizes. Although the core activity is still donation in cash or kind, other activities are becoming well-established and there are benefits for the companies concerned as well as the community.

- There are no areas of activity that are the sole preserve of the well-established corporate donors: the range of companies involved is so varied that there is scope for companies of all kinds to learn from the good practice examples cited in this report and in other recent studies.

- Small and medium-sized firms experience more constraints on time, financial resources and staffing than larger ones, and are not as active in community support as large companies, but there is considerable scope for more involvement. There is particular scope for a positive role for small companies in school links, local recruitment, employee volunteering, training initiatives and local investment.

The next section looks at the organisational underpinning of good practice. What forms of organisation and policy facilitate good practices of the kind outlined above?

3.3 Organisational issues for companies
We asked companies and other bodies about several important issues for management of community investment: control of budgets and decision-making; the existence of corporate policy; and the relationship between central headquarters and local managers.

Budgets and decision making
For cash donations, many firms operated a charitable donations budget, often controlled by a board member or board committee. Sponsorship cash was generally controlled by marketing or public relations departments. In larger firms, school links and training initiatives were often under the management of the personnel function. In the large companies with major community involvement programmes, there was often a community relations or corporate affairs department with full-time specialist staff; this department would operate the charities budget, organise secondments, and

administer company policy on community involvement. In some cases this operation had become a separate division of the company – as in the case of Grand Metropolitan Community Services Limited and Barclays Community Enterprise. Large firms sometimes also operated a separate company foundation through which all charitable monies passed. Within small and medium-sized firms there was no room for separate departments for community affairs, or for full-time staff dedicated to community investment; decision making resided with board members in most cases, with some part-time support from other staff.

The budget to be spent was decided at board level in all cases, but the true overall level of spending within many firms is very hard to assess, as emphasised by other recent work on company organisation for community involvement. The time spent by staff in volunteering schemes, on secondments, school liaison and other forms of employee activity was rarely costed and included in assessments of overall spending. This was true of firms of all sizes.

It could be argued that the common separation of budgets for charitable giving and other forms of support from 'mainstream' line departments suggests that community investment is marginalised as an activity in many firms, or is the preserve of the chairman or chief executive. This is no doubt true in some cases, but the existence of distinct departments, divisions or foundations for administering community budgets among the major corporate donors does not mean that they are necessarily cut off from the mainstream of the company's activities. Provided that good links are forged with the line departments for information exchange and liaison on activities which concern them (for instance, with Personnel in relation to secondment), there is no reason why setting up a community affairs department should lead to the marginalisation of community affairs. Within smaller firms, with shorter lines of communication, the scope for liaison of this kind between the controller of a 'community budget' should be no less than in large companies.

The company interviews we carried out, and other recent research, indicate that the key organisational issue is not so much the budgetary arrangements but rather how far companies have a *policy* on community involvement which has committed support from the board, shapes decisions over budgets and organisational structures and provides a message about the level of importance attached to community investment by the organisation.

Corporate policy for community investment

The findings of recent studies (Fogarty and Christie, 1991; Action Resource Centre, 1989; Metcalf, Pearson and Martin, 1989) indicate that there is a widespread lack of well thought-out and coherent policies among companies involved in community support of different kinds. In their review of charitable job creation schemes, Metcalf et al found that many companies lacked strategy in their activities, often working in an ad hoc manner and highly dependent on the initiative and enthusiasm of particular individuals. Action Resource Centre, in a survey of secondment practices, identified a general lack of policy for evaluation of benefits and management of secondees. Fogarty and Christie, in a survey of 120 medium-sized companies, found that nearly 70 per cent had no formal written policy on company donations and community involvement; that most were reliant on applications from charities and community groups for information on needs; and that few were able to break down their overall estimate for expenditure on community support into amounts for particular types of activity. The dominant policy style appears to be ad hoc and reactive, with companies responding to requests from the community while having no firm and considered basis for decisions on how much to spend, what to support and why.

Our interviews in the three cities confirmed the overall picture of a lack of focus and coherent policy among many firms, particularly, but by no means exclusively, amomg small and medium-sized companies. However, where companies were more conscious of the long-range benefits of community support to the firm, as well as of their corporate social responsibility, there tended to be more effective policy development and management of community support. This is not to say that philanthropic motivation means lack of policy: as noted in Chapter 2 above, enlightened self-interest and a developed sense of good corporate citizenship go hand in hand in many cases. However, it is clear that philanthropic giving often takes place without benefit of clear objectives and policies in many companies. There are good reasons, from the company and community point of view, for paying attention to the development of a corporate policy on community investment.

Good practice in policy development

The companies which appeared to recipients of support, inter-mediaries and their own staff to be acting most effectively in the community were those which had developed a coherent policy for their activities. This took many different forms, from a broad 'mission statement' on company values and community involvement, to detailed guidelines for managers on what to spend, how to spend it and which areas were to be supported. In those firms which appeared to be most successful in their community investment, having a policy did not mean being tied down to a fixed pattern of organisation and a rigid set of criteria for support: rather, it meant that there was commitment among senior management to community involvement as an integral part of the company's work; mechanisms for reaching decisions on what to support, and criteria for guidance; mechanisms for involving staff throughout the company; and mechanisms for delivering resources to the community in a flexible, coherent and proactive fashion.

What are the advantages which flow from the development of a well thought-out corporate policy? Benefits can be identified for the company and the community.

Targeting resources

Perhaps the key factor is that a clear corporate policy allows a focus for the allocation of resources. Many companies spoke of the 'flood' of requests for charitable support which flowed in; given limited resources, it is essential to devise criteria for decisions about support, or else companies may become wholly reactive and ad hoc in their giving, relying on the preferences of an individual (such as the chairman) and unable to judge the value of what they are doing either for the recipients or the company. As one manager put it, 'It is very easy to give money away; it is more difficult to make it truly effective'. Without a policy to focus the activity, company support is likely to be ad hoc and often ineffectual.

Targeting of resources does not simply bring clarity to decision making over what to support and what to turn down. It also means that more resources can be brought to bear on the specific areas identified for support than if small sums are scattered among many organisations. It is true, as several respondents said, that relatively small sums can go a long way in many voluntary bodies; but it is likely that more targeting will make more of an impact on recipients not only in terms of the amounts involved but also in terms of the relationship that may be developed with donor companies.

Among the companies visited the areas of focus varied widely: for small firms the target might be the local schools and charities; among larger national firms there might be a range of areas of interest, each with their own allocation from the overall budget for community investment – this is the pattern among organisations such as IBM, British Telecom and Grand Metropolitan Community Services. Typically, guidelines advise avoidance of political and religious causes, and frequently companies decline to become involved in obtaining basic equipment and facilities for schools and hospitals, regarding these as the responsibility of the public sector.

The process of devising a focussed policy also helps companies recognise what their strengths are and how to put them to best use in community action. This can mean linking support to areas related to the company's business and fields of expertise. A good example is provided by Hewlett Packard in Bristol, where the first priority is making use of the company's central area of expertise, information technology; next, donating company equipment; and finally, making cash donations.

Targeting more resources on a selected number of areas for support may also give more scope for long-term core funding of community ventures: although one-off contributions and project-based funding are valuable, recipients stressed the importance of a continuing flow of support which provided a secure basis for planning and development. The same point is made in recent Department of Environment studies of good practice in urban regeneration programmes (see Appendix 4). A 'more for less' policy of targeting resources clearly gives companies more potential for considering this kind of continuing support.

Message to the community
The existence of a clearly focussed policy provides a message to voluntary bodies about the scope of a company's activities and may help to avoid approaches from organisations which stand no chance of support. It also provides a message to employees, prospective recruits, customers and shareholders about the firm's commitment to community investment: as we saw in Chapter 2 above, this may

become a significant factor in companies' success in the labour and consumer markets in coming years. As noted by a manager of an industry-education links programme in a Bristol company, the existence of a public statement of policy also 'anchors' the commitment to support and offers some security against reduction of resources in a commercial downturn: having a policy statement 'means that we've set the precedent now – there's no turning back'. Obviously there can be no guarantee of the commitment to community involvement come what may – financial circumstances are naturally the ultimate constraint on activity, and if a firm falls on hard times then support is likely to be cut; however, the embedding of community support in a policy statement offers a significant level of 'protection' for the company's commitment.

Putting a value on activities
Without a coherent policy it is hard for companies to develop mechanisms for obtaining best value from their activities, for communities as well as for themselves. These include procedures for monitoring what is spent, following up projects in the community to assess the successes and problems of particular activities, developing effective and long-term links with community bodies, managing secondment schemes effectively, and assessing the overall value of community contributions. This last point is important, as without a policy to underpin the management of community investment, information needed to assess effectiveness of activities may not be collected, and the full value of company activity may not be reported. As we saw in Chapter 2, available statistics on company giving are flawed by serious underestimates of expenditure in areas such as secondment. Without procedures for assessing and reporting the full value of contributions, companies and their employees are unlikely to gain due acknowledgement of their activities in the community.

Involving the whole company
Our case studies, and those of other recent researchers, underlined the vital role played by accident and 'catalysing' personalities in company support for the community. Often a firm becomes involved in forms of support through chance encounters or individuals' determination. The role played by 'crusading' individuals is crucial to the continuing dynamism of company action, but there is a danger that, once they

move on within the firm or leave, momentum will be lost. The development of clear policy can reduce the risk of over-dependence on key individuals by establishing mechanisms for decision making and management for community support which bring in other people and parts of the organisation: for example, a Community Affairs department linked to the board and to line departments; a special committee of the main board which involves all key line departments; a committee which brings in employee representatives as well as senior managers. We have come across successful examples of all of these systems, and all underpin, and in turn are underpinned by, a clear statement of policy on community investment.

Respondents in well-established Community Affairs departments or divisions in large companies stress the importance of linking the traditional 'charitable donations' budget with activities related to mainstream departments, such as secondments, sponsorship and training initiatives. In companies such as Grand Metropolitan Community Services and British Telecom, charitable donations are one strand of a multi-faceted overall organisation for management of community support. In principle this kind of integration should be easier for small firms to achieve as they move from simple donations towards more proactive and varied forms of support, since lines of communication and responsibility are so much shorter than in large companies.

The importance of commitment at board level to policy is evident if community activities are to be well-resourced and managed, and this point was often made. The importance to many companies of activating employee enthusiasm and participation was also often underlined. A point which is less often heard, but which is very important, is the need for commitment to be secured at middle management levels and in the regional and local organisation of national companies. One secondee to a promotional body from a leading financial organisation noted that the backing she received from her board was excellent, but that there was widespread incomprehension among middle management of her motivation for taking on the secondment and lack of understanding of its role in company policy on community action and management development. In large firms, the existence of a committed and enlightened board is not enough: policy needs to ensure that the message on the importance of community investment goes all the way down.

Relationship between central management and local action

This leads us to consideration of a key aspect of organisational policy in relation to community support: the balance between central management of resources and local needs. Several respondents argued that centralisation of resources in national headquarters and a lack of autonomy in decisions on community support in regions and localities was poor practice. It meant that national promotions and appeals typically received large scale support, while local initiatives were starved of funds and autonomy. One manager of a local branch of a national company noted that central budgets for sponsorship were enormously greater than those allocated to him for community action in an inner city area, although he felt that the benefit to the community and company of increasing resources for local action would outweigh those gained from national promotions.

Several company informants said that it was policy to avoid subscribing to large national appeals, which tended to be able 'to take care of themselves'. There needed to be more priority for potentially 'unpopular' or relatively obscure causes which demanded support at local level. One chief executive of a chamber of commerce argued powerfully against community investment policies decided in London which set an inflexible policy for local management and could not allow decision makers to 'get the feel for real issues'. It could also delay decisions unnecessarily if control was over-concentrated at the centre. Community investment had to be locally managed with effective local budgets, since local conditions varied so much and grassroots knowledge was essential to success. Good practice was considered to involve a broad and coherent central policy, with devolution of adequate budgets to regional departments and local branch management as well as a degree of flexible autonomy in selecting initiatives to support within the overall policy framework. Major firms which were cited as examples of this kind of good practice by respondents included Marks & Spencer, IBM, Grand Metropolitan, Barclays and British Telecom. For smaller firms which might feel that the practice of giant corporations in community involvement is irrelevant to their circumstances and resources, there may be much to learn from local management policies in firms such as BT and IBM, which at the local branch level are effectively medium-sized companies.

Respondents also noted the powerful effect of committed companies which had their headquarters outside London and which had a policy of local targeting of activity: for instance, Granada and Kellogg in Manchester (and the North West region more generally), and IMI in Birmingham.

The specific problems of inner city areas and the demands of local economic and environmental regeneration call for substantial commitment of resources and for considerable local knowledge among companies seeking to get involved. This argues for wider practice of flexible policies among London-based national companies in particular, which may need to consider how to allocate significant resources and autonomy to local management, or target central resources directly on local areas with high levels of need.

The important point about the role of awareness of and responsiveness to local conditions raises the question of linkages between companies and the community. Good practice does not simply relate to how companies develop their policy and organise their community involvement. It also concerns the integration of companies into networks and partnerships which can greatly enhance the value of their activities. This is the subject of the next section.

3.4 Networks and partnerships

Most of the major companies contacted in the course of the research are members of national promotional initiatives such as Business in the Community and the Per Cent Club. They were also generally well connected at local level with public sector bodies and initiatives linking community goups and the private sector. However, links between small and medium-sized companies and national and local agencies or networks were less frequent – a finding confirmed in Fogarty and Christie (1991) and in interviews with managers in intermediary bodies at national and local level. Small and medium-sized firms were also less likely to be involved in partnership ventures with bodies from other sectors.

It is useful to devise a framework for understanding the various kinds of partnership which arise in business involvement in the community. We can distinguish three levels of partnership activity:

- direct links between the firm and the community;
- multi-firm groupings;
- partnerships between private, public and voluntary sector bodies.

These different levels of activity are by no means mutually exclusive; on the contrary, many companies, principally large ones, are involved in all three. Examples of good practice in each area are given below.

Direct links between firms and the community

Clearly any form of charitable donation from a company involves some form of direct link with the community. However, there need not be any kind of continuing relationship beyond the receipt of a thank-you letter from the recipient. A more interactive, lasting relationship or partnership between the individual firm and community bodies may result, however, from the development of a more focussed policy on company involvement, especially where companies go beyond cash giving and begin to devote time and expertise to community bodies.

Examples can be multiplied from around the country. Among smaller firms, the development of special links with local schools, hospitals or other organisations important to employees and other local people was common. In the case of Clayton Aniline in East Manchester, the policy of focussing support on the local community includes preparation and distribution of a quarterly newsletter on company developments and local activities such as school events to 9,000 local homes. There are numerous examples from our case study cities of fruitful direct links in areas such as training and employment support initiatives, and support for small businesses and enterprise agencies.

The benefits from forming a closer attachment are numerous. Those identified by respondents include improved communications with local community groups, potential benefit for the company from goodwill and favourable publicity, and opportunities for local recruitment. Employees are also more likely to be activated into supporting local causes than more remote national ones, and direct special relationships with schools and other local bodies can increase employees' interest in community involvement. Lasting links provide a focus for company activity, and allow more opportunity for monitoring progress and ensuring that ventures are successful.

Multi-firm groupings

There are many different cases of activities carried out by companies working in concert, or by business associations. Chambers of Commerce may be especially active and effective in forming community links in some localities – the Birmingham chamber was singled out by informants in that city. There are many positive examples of multi-firm groupings, and a number stand out in our case study cities. In Bristol the Traders' Association, comprising around 100 firms from the Brislington Trading Estate, has formed links with local schools in an employer-led initiative. In Birmingham the Ten Companies Group collaborates on equal opportunities initiatives targeted on ethnic minority communities. In Manchester there is a 'Business Support Group' which brings 13 companies together to contribute to initiatives for the regeneration of the local economy in Moss Side and Hulme. In Birmingham the Business Action Team brings together seconded staff from a number of companies to offer support to small firms in danger of bankruptcy. All of these deserve study outside the cities in question and may offer good models for wider development of multi-firm links with communities.

A looser form of inter-firm activity is the establishment of Per Cent Clubs, which bring together companies nationwide and in two localities so far (Sheffield and Newcastle). The clubs are not sources of funds, nor do they lay down any policy direction for their members. Their role is to provide firms with a yardstick for community contributions: membership of the national club means a public commitment to dedicating 0.5 per cent of pre-tax profits to community involvement in whatever form the company wishes. In the local clubs, the commitment is to allocate up to 1 per cent of locally-generated pre-tax profits. The target percentage for Per Cent Club members is now set to rise to 1 per cent by 1992. So far there are no Per Cent Clubs in our three case study cities.

Companies in partnership with public and voluntary sector bodies

Individual firms and multi-firm partnerships are frequently involved in wider collaborations which bring together other companies, business organisations, and bodies from the public and voluntary sector. There are several types of partnership, as outlined below.

Links between companies and the community may be mediated by a 'broker' such as a community trust, Business in the Community or Action Resource Centre (ARC). ARC, for example, acts as an intermediary in identifying for companies opportunities for secondments and short-term assignments of staff, and assisting in the management of secondments. For large companies with considerable expertise in community links and with many community contacts, the use of intermediaries may be relatively infrequent, although we came across numerous examples of partnership.

For small and medium-sized firms with less in-house expertise in community action than major companies, and less experience in dealing with community groups, the formation of partnership with intermediaries can be of great value. In Bristol, the case of Mosaic offers the example to small firms of how a partnership with a community trust can help significantly in the development of a policy for involvement. The company has linked up with the Greater Bristol Trust (GBT), whose director forwards details of projects which fit the company's criteria for support, and to which most of the company's community budget goes for distribution to causes via GBT grants. The arrangement contributes towards GBT's endowment, allows the company to identify projects it wants to support, and saves staff time in responding to requests and investigating projects.

A second type of partnership is a link between companies and public sector bodies and community groups or individuals in the delivery of publicly funded initiatives. The most important example of private-public partnership at present is the establishment of the new TECs and LECs for development of local training programmes and enterprise support schemes. Many of the companies visited for this study were getting involved at different levels in their local TECs. Other examples of joint activity involved the government's inner city Task Forces, which in all three cities were engaged in various projects linking companies with the community; and collaborations with local authorities and government agencies in targeted training initiatives to equip local people for employment. A notable example of partnership in the inner city is provided in Moss Side in Manchester, where the Business Support Group mentioned above is working alongside the local Task Force, the Community Development Trust, and the local enterprise agency, and where business support is spread across the two community agencies.

A new development which appears to promise much and could be the model for further partnership agreements is the recent 'Working

Partnership' initiative between the government's Action for Cities programme and the Institute of Personnel Management. The IPM will be working in inner city areas with the government's City Action Teams and Task Forces, and with local TECs, to help develop schemes for pre-recruitment training, targeted recruitment and school-industry links. This initiative should improve communications between the CATs, Task Forces and the private sector, and brings 'mainstream' management in the form of personnel managers into the community involvement scene in inner city areas. If the initiative succeeds, it could be a useful model for similar schemes to bring other line management functions into community programmes to a greater extent than at present: one area which could benefit from such an approach is the promotion of local purchasing agreements in inner city areas.

A third form of partnership involves strategic bodies linking business leaders with local authorities, higher education, public authorities and bodies such as urban development corporations. One model for this form of partnership is the Business Leadership Team (BLT), pioneered in Newcastle and promoted in the CBI report 'Initiatives Beyond Charity' in 1988. BLTs have been established in several areas, including Bristol (the Bristol Initiative), the North West, Sheffield and Blackburn. BLTs have been concerned with city-wide or regional investment, especially in major infrastructural and training projects, and with coordination of activities between leading actors from different sectors in their areas. There is obviously an overlap between the concerns and aims of BLTs and TECs, and in areas where both exist there is frequent overlapping in board membership to ensure good coordination. In Birmingham, partnership at the strategic level has taken the form of the Birmingham Heartlands venture, a collaborative initiative between the city council, chamber of commerce, and major companies for development of the inner city economy – in effect, a non-statutory urban development corporation.

Finally, there are other formal and informal networks which bring actors from different organisations and sectors together. The Common Purpose initiative (see Chapter 2) being established currently in many parts of the UK aims to facilitate the creation of local networks of 'leaders' from different walks of life in the community. At the operational level, there are moves in Bristol and Sheffield to establish networks of organisations involved in giving grants and other forms of support to groups in the community; as with Common Purpose, these networks bring people together, from local authority departments, voluntary bodies and companies, who might never meet otherwise.

The benefits from partnership and networking
Going beyond a simple policy of reacting to requests for support is not without its problems for companies. Developing community links, and then moving into networks with other companies and bodies from the public and voluntary sector, are unfamiliar activities for many firms. Networking and building partnerships are time-consuming. Companies may often need the assistance of intermediaries such as BitC or ARC, and need to exercise diplomacy and tact in forming partnership ventures: as one respondent emphasised, many managers see their firm as the natural 'leader' in a partnership initiative, and everyone will need to be given some sense of 'ownership' if bruised egos are to be avoided and maximum commitment obtained. Moreover, there are likely to be misunderstandings and 'cultural' clashes on the way to fruitful partnership with community groups, which may be suspicious of the private sector and as unfamiliar with the idea of collaborative work as the companies. Nonetheless, many respondents in companies, intermediary bodies and community groups stressed that the partnership approach to company investment brought significant benefits to all concerned:

- As one informant put it, 'two plus two can equal five': partnerships can lead to a pooling of ideas and experience which create a 'synergy' from the interaction of organisations and individuals. In the context of urban renewal, the complexity and interlocking nature of the problems mean that no single organisation is able to bring to bear the full range of skills and resources required. Partnerships can lead to information exchange, transfer of skills, and a form of creative 'brainstorming'.
- Partnership approaches involving intermediary bodies can facilitate the development of fruitful links between companies and the community, and, as in the case of community trusts, save time in identifying projects to support – especially valuable to small and medium-sized firms with no staff to spare for a distinct community affairs function.
- Partnerships allow member organisations to enter each other's networks of contacts, and this is also a potential source of

'synergy' and the development of new ideas. Via partnerships, individual organisations can gain access to networks of leaders in their local community and gain a city-wide or regional perspective which they could not otherwise obtain. Moreover, partnership ventures form a network in their own right for other groups to contact and tap, and can develop a role in 'signposting' – passing on enquiries from outside bodies and referring them to other sources of information.

- As one community affairs manager said, once a company, however sophisticated its community programmes, seeks to enter areas beyond its own expertise, it needs to get involved in forms of partnership in order to add value to its contributions. For example, his company wished to go beyond established programmes in charitable giving, training and volunteering and make a contribution to tackling homelessness; this was so large and complex an area that the only way to get started was to enter into collaborations with other companies and with public and voluntary sector agencies.

- Finally, many respondents made the very important point that companies and public agencies cannot impose 'solutions' on local communities, especially in areas with complex interlocking problems such as inner cities. For initiatives to succeed, a 'gift' relationship with the local community is not enough: there has to be real collaboration in designing and implementing initiatives for the local economy and community, and the voice of local people has to be heard.

Key messages on good practice

The case studies and other recent research reveal many striking cases of company investment in the community, and these should offer encouragement to currently uncommitted firms to join in. Key messages on practice are as follows:

- Good practice is associated with development of coherent company policy on community investment: policy provides the essential basis for setting priorities, assessing budget levels, selecting causes to support, involving employees and developing a proactive approach which can maximise benefits for the community and potentially bring long-term advantages to the company.

- Although the community investment world is dominated by major corporations, there is considerable scope for effective community action by small and medium-sized firms, especially in areas such as school-industry links, support in cash and kind, local recruitment and provision of expert advice.
- Entry into networks and partnerships of companies, public agencies and voluntary groups can lead to effective development of community investment initiatives and provide valuable means of information exchange, development of new skills, and link individual organisations with city-wide or regional leaders.

There is widespread agreement among respondents in all sectors on these good practice points. There is also a high degree of consensus on the obstacles to bringing more companies into the culture of community investment and spreading good practice. In the next section we examine the main obstacles and look at possible ways of overcoming them suggested by the city case studies and other recent research.

4 Overcoming Obstacles to Implementation of Good Practice

What were the obstacles to good practice in community involvement identified by respondents in companies and in other organisations? In this chapter we examine the main problems highlighted in the course of the city case studies and discussions with informants at national level in companies, public agencies and intermediary bodies. We also put forward recommendations for action in overcoming these obstacles: in many cases these have been suggested by successful or at least promising new initiatives in the cities visited, by informants in companies, public bodies or community organisations, or by study of other recent research.

The sections below deal with the following broad areas in which obstacles need to be overcome:

- improving company organisation and policy development;
- raising management awareness and recruiting more firms into the culture of community involvement;
- building partnerships involving the private sector;
- improving networks and coordination of initiatives and information.

4.1 Organisational problems

Chapter 3 identified good practice in internal organisation in companies as being associated with the development of coherent policies on community investment which allow firms to set priorities for funding, judge the level of commitment they wish to make, evaluate progress and develop community links. The difficulties with statistical information on company giving, and the widespread complaints that many firms are insufficiently focussed in their community activities, indicate a need to improve company policy making. How can this be done?

Expenditure on community investment

Fogarty and Christie (1991) make recommendations for new requirements on the reporting of community expenditure by companies, which should improve the collection and presentation of statistical data on what is spent by companies and on which areas. The standardisation of reporting of community contributions has been promoted by Charities Aid Foundation and the Per Cent Club; a voluntary code of practice is needed to encourage declarations on a standard basis.

We heard from some respondents that many companies are beginning to pay close attention to the reporting of community investment by the major company contributors, who often produce comprehensive separate reports on their activities. A stimulus to better collection and reporting of data should improve existing peer group competition in this area, as well as provide much more accurate information to the public, to charities and community groups, to shareholders, employees and not least to senior managers themselves about what they are actually spending.

There is a need to provide firms with clear yardsticks on the level of expenditure which can reasonably be expected of good corporate citizens. Mosaic in Bristol may be unique in setting a level of 10 per cent of pre-tax profits ('Big enough to make a difference'), and will be exceptional for a long time; however, many companies could do much more than they do at present in terms of percentage contributions without causing problems for shareholders. Fogarty and Christie (1991) found that companies interviewed and surveyed about the potential constraints on community contributions did not rank shareholder opposition as a very important factor; the level of contributions at which shareholders might express anxiety would seem to lie well beyond even that of the most active and generous leading companies. The role of the Per Cent Club in establishing a widely accepted yardstick – originally 0.5 per cent of pre-tax profits, and rising to 1 per cent by 1992 – is important in this context. The setting of a figure to which many firms subscribe publicly and that is clearly acceptable to shareholders gives companies outside the culture something to latch on to. The Per Cent Club needs to be marketed more powerfully in the UK, both nationally and locally, via the creation of more local clubs as in Newcastle and Sheffield.

Company policy making

Effective action in the community needs to be based on a clear view of what the company wishes to achieve, what its priorities are for support, how its efforts are to be led, evaluated and communicated, and how staff at all levels are to be involved. All too often companies have no clear policies on community action, and their involvement is ad hoc, reactive and unfocussed, leading to less than optimum results for community causes and for the business. There is a great need for more companies to develop more systematic policies to guide their community investment.

Some helpful material already exists on how to devise company policy on aspects of community investment: the publications of Directory of Social Change and the Council for Charitable Support offer comprehensive guides to the corporate contributor to the community, but they are very little used by businesses. Promotional and intermediary bodies such as BitC, Community Development Foundation and ARC have produced helpful guidelines for policy on community investment in general and on particular forms of investment such as secondment; these need to be given as wide a circulation as possible. The promotional bodies have expertise which is put to use in the form of consultancy to their members and clients; these services need to be more widely publicised.

On policy development generally, the dissemination of good practice is crucial. Reports may help to some extent, but there is also a need for more direct communication of success stories and lessons for practitioners. There is a role here for business schools, in partnership with leading companies or promotional bodies, to organise conferences, seminars and workshops for the exchange of ideas among companies already involved in the community and newcomers to the field.

Michael Norton of Directory of Social Change has also suggested that Community Affairs managers within the leading companies should form a professional association, through which good practice could be disseminated, quality standards discussed, and information exchanged. This idea certainly seems worth following up among community affairs professionals, who already have an informal forum, the Corporate Responsibility Group. One role for such an association would be to promote training and accreditation of community affairs staff. Other suggestions in this area which deserve further attention include more appointments or secondments into companies from the voluntary sector, public agencies involved in urban renewal, and community groups; and secondments of company staff to voluntary bodies or other community organisations before taking up community affairs responsibilities. A further idea is suggested by the success of the management courses for the voluntary sector run by IBM; a variation on such courses, run by an individual company, group of companies, or by an association of community affairs professionals, could be devised to disseminate skills in management of community involvement programmes.

One area where more information is needed on how best to organise community investment is the relationship between central/national policy within companies and local activity. Several respondents felt that many companies were over-centralised, London-focussed and unduly rigid in their policies, and that effective community investment, especially in inner city areas, demanded greater autonomy for local managers and increased devolution of budgets. The good practice model seems to be one of 'thinking globally, acting locally': setting a comprehensive policy line at the top, but allowing considerable devolution of resources and a degree of flexibility in interpretation at local level of overall policy. Many companies could usefully consider how far they could increase the value of their community activities both to communities and to themselves by decentralising budgets and reponsibility to a greater extent. As some informants noted, local links were the key to activating employees' enthusiasm; and as one local manager argued, transfer of resources from national sponsorship budgets to local community action budgets might result in more benefits for firms as well as for local people. The whole area of national-local links deserves a fuller debate and more study and exchange of ideas between practitioners: it should be taken up by BitC and its partners in the Bridge Group of promotional agencies, and calls for high level debate between practitioners – for example, as an early debate within any new association of community affairs professionals.

4.2 Raising management awareness and recruiting companies into the culture

Although there are many cases of good practice to be found in community involvement by companies, it is clear that a great many companies are engaged only at a low level, if at all. In attempting to develop partnerships with the private sector, respondents from community bodies, City Action Teams and Task Forces frequently encountered apathy, vagueness about possibilities for action, and lack of awareness of problems and information sources. Many firms have yet to develop their activities beyond reacting in ad hoc fashion to requests for charitable donations. The good practices mentioned in this report are characteristic of the major firms with established community action programmes and of many smaller firms which have entered the culture of community investment; these companies are as yet very much in the minority, and of course few would argue that there is no room for substantial further development among the acknowledged leaders in community investment. There is scope for more development in terms of the proportion of pre-tax profits dedicated to community investment and in the broadening of activities beyond traditional financial support.

However, as several respondents said, there are now so many demands on companies' resources, and so much exhortation on all sides to contribute more to the community and the environment, that 'donor fatigue' and 'saturation' are in the air. The onset of a sharp recession in the economy in late 1990 also threatened to lead to cuts in companies' contributions and a check to the momentum built up over the past decade by the community investment movement in the UK. Statistics are not yet available on the pattern of expenditure for 1990/91 but it is likely that many firms' contributions will have fallen as a result of the recession. This makes the identification of ways of overcoming obstacles all the more important. Problems and possible means of tackling them are examined below.

Developing 'champions'

One difficulty in drawing more companies into the culture is the fact that much depends on the existence within them of individuals who are able to push the arguments forward at senior levels and develop policies with determination and enthusiasm. 'Champions' of any new activity are rare within organisations, and any initiative which could develop more business leaders with enthusiasm for community links needs to be pursued urgently. A promising development at present is the establishment of Common Purpose in many cities around the UK. This initiative aims to build up cadres of local leaders from all walks of life who, after a common training course and exposure to each other's working worlds and problems, should form a powerful community network. BitC has also developed schemes to promote the development of 'champions', for example its Business Leadership Programme run in 1990.

Smaller firms and Per Cent Clubs

The community investment scene is dominated by major companies, but there is much scope, as we have seen, for activity by small and medium-sized companies, not just in charitable giving but also in school-industry links, targeted training and recruitment, and potentially also in local purchasing initiatives. BitC in the North West has run a campaign to raise awareness among small and medium-sized firms, which until now have not been a priority for promotional organisations; this is scheduled to run on a nationwide basis over the next three years, albeit on a limited scale.

Another initiative which some informants saw as a good vehicle for drawing smaller firms into the culture of involvement is the development of local Per Cent Clubs. So far these only exist in Newcastle and Sheffield. Per Cent Clubs act as a means of signalling business commitment, and are a relatively inexpensive means of recruiting companies and generating interest in localities. The local focus may well appeal more to potential members than the more 'remote' nature of the national Per Cent Club. The establishment of Per Cent Clubs also provides companies with a widely accepted yardstick for judging how much to contribute to the community; provides a focus for peer group pressure and exchange of experience; and creates a new local network for employers and for community bodies to use. We recommend that BitC and the national Per Cent Club review local experience to date in Newcastle and Sheffield, with a view to setting up local clubs on a nationwide basis. It could be useful to give priority to cities targeted in the government's Action for Cities programme. None of our case study cities has a Per Cent Club, but all could benefit from the interest it would generate.

Consultancy on corporate policy

The business of reaching out to smaller companies, and indeed to large firms not involved in community support, is time-consuming and difficult. However, there is no ready substitute for the hard work of making personal contacts and 'evangelising' companies at the top. As underlined in Fogarty and Christie (1991), many respondents in business and in the voluntary sector see a need for more personnel and capital resources for marketing of community investment by promotional agencies and intermediaries such as community trusts. These bodies are stretched in terms of staffing and finance and more resources are required if a larger marketing effort is to be made and if promotional initiatives are to be followed up effectively. As an economic downturn sets in after the boom years of the 1980s, it is important to ensure that the momentum built up over the last decade does not fade away; in this respect there may be a case for more public 'pump-priming' funds to be made available as an investment in raising awareness among companies of the scope for involvement in the community. In particular, as noted in Chapter 3, there is a need for more coherent policy development, and companies may often need expert guidance in doing this and setting priorities for action which reflect community needs and company strengths. What measures could be devised to meet this need?

One innovation which could serve the purpose of a) focussing on the needs of smaller companies in relation to community investment, b) improving company policies, c) raising awareness of the promotional bodies' services, and d) providing them with more resources, would be the introduction of *government grants for consultancy on community investment*. Grants for consultancy are a well-established part of the government's Enterprise Initiative: up to two-thirds of the cost of 5 to 15 days of consultancy for firms with under 500 employees is paid for in the fields of marketing, design, business planning, manufacturing systems, quality management and information systems. Grants for consultancy in community investment could be introduced, under a separate scheme, on the lines of those made under the Enterprise Initiative, following the existing pattern: small and medium-sized companies could obtain part funding of consultancy fees for services from approved consultants – in this case, one would expect the established promotional agencies to be on the 'approved' list. Such a measure might also serve to encourage more business schools to develop research, training and consultancy expertise in the field of community investment. Consultancy projects would cover internal organisational questions, development of corporate policy, links with community bodies, and development of partnership ventures. We feel that this recommendation could receive wide support, and hope that it will be debated by the promotional agencies and Government departments. Whether or not this proposal is taken up and elaborated, however, there is a need for more general debate on means of securing more resources for marketing the message of community investment.

'Social awards' and company motivation

One informant noted the lack of 'social awards' for corporate action in the community and argued that more forms of public recognition of excellence would be helpful. There are numerous award schemes already for particular areas of activity – for example, Gardner Merchant is sponsoring awards over the next three years for the most successful industry-education partnerships; the Employment Department has a scheme of National Training Awards; and the TECs and LECs will be able to award 'kitemarks' to companies meeting high quality standards in training. A more generally-based award scheme exists, in the form of the Lord Mayor of London's 'Dragon Awards' for business involvement in the community. There could be merit, however, in taking up the idea suggested in the 1988 CBI report *Initiatives Beyond Charity* for a national award scheme. A National Award for Community Investment, strongly promoted and equivalent in status to designations such as the Queen's Awards for export and technological achievement, could be a significant innovation in raising business awareness and interest.

Providing 'ammunition'

As noted in Chapter 1, there are difficulties in providing 'ammunition', especially in the form of well-founded statistics, about the positive benefits which can flow to companies as well as communities from business action. This is because of the newness of so many of the initiatives, and the lack of adequate procedures in many firms for evaluating their activities and monitoring progress of projects which they support. Promotional bodies need more examples of good practice and success stories which are potentially reproducible, from around the UK and also from the rest of the European Community, which has been neglected as a source of examples in favour of the USA in recent years. There is a role here for business schools and business umbrella groups to do more research and to publicise the results.

The role of management education
More generally, a number of respondents have noted the lack in the UK of a coherent body of management theory on the whole field of corporate social responsibility. So far, management schools have not developed courses which take a comprehensive view of the subject, embracing business ethics, environmental responsibility and community action. Much more activity is needed in course design and research in order to bring out the connections between mainstream business concerns and social responsibility – for example, in relation to the link made by one of our informants between his firm's policy on total quality management and its involvement in community support. Business schools also have a role to play in raising awareness among the rising generation of managers, and more concentration of issues of social responsibility in management education should in principle lead to more socially responsible managers in the future.

The recent establishment by Manchester Business School, under the leadership of Professor Tom Cannon, of the Co-Operative Bank Chair in Corporate Responsibility, is an example of good practice which deserves to be followed up in other business schools. Manchester will be setting up an institute for research into corporate social responsibility, and this should become a focus for involvement of the private sector and other groups in conferences, seminars and debates on policy and good practice. Such a unit should also have an important part to play in provision of consultancy to the private and voluntary sector on community involvement by business. Professor Cannon has been involved in work in Manchester with public and voluntary agencies in the inner city areas, and with firms such as Kellogg and Marks & Spencer on aspects of community investment. This form of activity in relation to community involvement deserves emulation in other management schools, as does the incorporation of a course on corporate responsibility into the Master's in Business Administration (MBA) syllabus at Manchester. The establishment of two or more further chairs and/or research units in corporate social responsibility, and the inclusion of the subject in all MBA courses and degree courses in business studies and related subjects, would be significant steps in promoting the culture of community investment and good corporate citizenship.

Balance of public and private funding in the community

What is the proper balance between private and public sector support for community initiatives and services? This question raises problems for the intermediary agencies, government and the private sector alike.

There is widespread concern among companies over the requests received for contributions to schools and hospitals for basic equipment, and a feeling among some that the private sector is too often called upon to pay for items and activities which should be the responsibility of the public purse. This feeling can only contribute to the danger of 'fatigue' and a sense of 'saturation' among companies faced with many demands on their time, resources and attention from initiatives such as TECs, school-business links and requests for charitable support. There is clearly a risk that companies might be deterred from developing a programme for investment in the community by resentment of what is perceived to be a withdrawal by the public sector from areas in which it has prime responsibility. Concern is also expressed by companies and voluntary groups that too much reliance on private sector support can place voluntary initiatives and services under strain: if core funding and long-term support are rarely available from the public sector, they are even less commonly provided by private sector contributors to the community.

There are no straightforward answers in this 'grey area'; there is a need for a continuing debate between business, intermediary agencies and government over the boundary between private and public responsibilities in community investment, and this is a topic which merits further investigation by agencies such as Business in the Community and the new research unit at Manchester Business School.

Involving customers and suppliers

Finally, there is the potential role of committed companies in spreading the message and good practice along their supply chains and in their own business networks to suppliers and customers. A few major firms such as Grand Metropolitan were involved to some extent in 'missionary' activity of this kind, but in general this was an underdeveloped area. Some respondents were reluctant to be seen as 'do-gooders', but a few expressed interest in encouraging suppliers to engage in community action. There is a link here with the point made by one company about the relationship between his firm's activity in the community and its overall strategy of total quality management (TQM). It is increasingly common for companies which have adopted TQM to enter into closer relationships with suppliers in order to help raise their quality standards as well, and in order to develop lasting links which will ensure continuity and reliability in supply. If community investment, and environmental protection policies also, are seen in the context of overall quality management – as they are in companies such as IBM – then there is scope for regarding them as elements of quality standards to be met by suppliers. This is an area which deserves more exploration by promotional bodies, business schools and above all by individual companies in their dealings with suppliers.

4.3 Building partnerships

Informants from all sectors emphasise the key role of the partnership approach in developing effective policies for action in community investment, especially in inner city areas. However, a number of political, organisational and 'cultural' obstacles are identified by many respondents. We examine these below and consider some possible ways of overcoming them.

The role of public agencies

First, there are complaints about the prevalence of 'short termism' among companies and government agencies. One fundamental point about urban renewal programmes in general, and about those centred on inner city problems in particular, is that they demand a long-term investment perspective. The scale of the problems is such that patience, readiness for a 'hard slog', commitment to funding initiatives over a long period and preparedness for risk-taking are all essential ingredients of action by the private and the public sector. We heard from numerous businessmen, community groups, promotional bodies and civil servants that government action is often not matching best practice by the private sector in this respect. Key problems identified by respondents are:

- the frequency, as businesses see it, of 'changes to the rules' in government programmes for funding of training and enterprise initiatives, which make planning and longer-term commitments more difficult;
- the short-term nature of project funding, which can run counter to the need to take 'measured risks', as one businessman put it, in inner city areas; there are also concerns over the short lifetimes of Task Forces and Urban Development Corporations and their capacity to provide for long-range initiatives which need continuity in funding and management support;
- confusion, 'jealousies and rivalries' between different departments and initiatives, which led one community affairs manager to conclude that it would often be better for companies to concentrate on inter-firm partnerships rather than working with public sector agencies;
- the complexity of government funding policies for urban renewal and the time-consuming nature of the effort to understand the rules and get involved with public bodies. One enterprise agency director said of the funding system for enterprise promotion, 'It took me six years to understand the mechanism'. One manager in Manchester said that many firms had no idea of how to obtain access to public funds to support their own inner city investment activities.

While we came across numerous examples of successful partnership between business and public agencies, there is obviously much room for improvement in the communication of policy to the private sector, for simplification of programmes and rules for funding, improved communication between departments, and above all a longer-term perspective on funding arrangements for inner city initiatives. This is especially important in the light of the sharp economic downturn experienced from late 1990 at the end of a long boom period in which the culture of community investment has developed strongly. A commitment to long-term thinking on investment by the public sector will play an important role in preventing any loss of momentum in the growth of community investment by business.

Cultural and political factors in the inner city

There are specific 'cultural' obstacles to the development of effective partnerships in the inner city. Mutual suspicion and incomprehension are likely at the outset of any initiative which aims to bring the private sector, public agencies and community groups together. This is especially the case in inner city areas which have been starved of investment and where community groups feel marginalised by society at large. The problems which companies and other bodies face include:

* the absence of any coherent umbrella organisation through which a community can make its voice heard: in areas such as Moss Side and Hulme there are many small community groups which may be highly fragmented and even hostile to one another;
* hostility to the private sector, suspicion of motives for getting involved, and lack of experience in dealing with companies;
* lack of skills and experience within the company in dealing with community groups;
* rivalries among the companies involved in a partnership;
* the danger of being seen to 'parachute in', as one informant put it, and try to impose solutions on a community;
* the need to adopt a long-term perspective and face up to a lengthy period of building trust and experimenting in partnership with community groups;
* the danger that initiatives for inner city areas may be too specifically targeted and have the effect, as one chief executive said, of 'building a wall' around the community. 'Problem' areas need above all to be reconnected with mainstream economic activity.

It would be remarkable if any local initiative for inner city renewal had managed to overcome all of these problems, given the relatively short time that many local partnership ventures have been in operation. However, one case stood out as an encouraging example of how progress can be made in an area with very severe economic and social problems: this is the example of Moss Side and Hulme in Manchester. Numerous attempts had been made in recent years by various agencies to stimulate new economic activity in this extremely disadvantaged area, but no systematic coordination of activity had taken place between the private and public sector and the community. Initiatives also foundered in the face of fragmentation of community groups and hostility to outside bodies arriving with 'solutions'. In 1989, after several years of independent involvement in the locality, Kellogg took the initiative in forming a partnership of locally-based companies which constituted a Business Support Group (BSG), a local spin-off from the Business Leadership Team for Manchester and the North West. The BSG is working in partnership with the new Community Development Trust, set up by the local Task Force, which provides a focus for community groups and partnership activity; this has four private sector trustees from the BSG. There is also an enterprise agency, AED, which is supported by BSG companies among others and works with the new Community Development Trust. There have been problems in communication and securing more business support and involvement from the local authority, but a start has been made which all parties agree is highly promising. What can other areas learn from this in overcoming cultural and political obstacles?

- The approach which has finally made an impact on the area was led by a strong local employer committed to a partnership with the public sector and community groups. The involvement of a major business was a key factor in securing cooperation from other firms.
- All the companies have an equal role in the BSG and all see prospects of medium- or long-term returns from their involvement for their business as well as for the community.
- The approach was systematic: it brought a number of companies together and integrated them in local initiatives – the Community Development Trust, the BSG and the local enterprise agency – and linked up with the local public sector agency, the Task Force.
- The initiative is founded on a clear declaration of policy (see the Manchester case study in Chapter 9) in the form of a charter for the BSG.
- The initiative equips Moss Side and Hulme with a 'triad' of key elements for economic and social regeneration. First, an enterprise agency; second, a forum for dialogue between community groups, business and the local authority, in the shape of the Community Development Trust; third, business support which is broadly-based and which connects the area with opportunities in the wider Manchester economy and with city-wide and regional networks such as the Business Leadership Team.

It is obviously too soon to judge the overall success of the Moss Side and Hulme partnership. However, the fact that so many participants view the recent developments as encouraging and positive should lead other areas to look at the experience and perhaps experiment in replacing parts of it.

Approaching business for support

If companies are frequently at a loss to know how to approach community groups, the feeling is often reciprocated. Moreover, among Task Forces as well there is no common strategy for getting the private sector involved in their inner city areas, although in Bristol and Moss Side and Hulme consultants were used in order to assist in the development of a local approach to business. The example of Moss Side and Hulme suggests that Task Forces should consider the use of Business Support Groups which can be linked to the Task Force, TECs, Business Leadership Teams or other appropriate local partnership agencies as a means of drawing in the private sector and connecting themselves and their areas to the wider business networks in their cities.

There is no ready solution to the problems which face community groups and voluntary organisations in knowing which firms to contact and how to deal with them. A key factor in the success of the recent initiatives in Moss Side seems to be the lead role played by a major firm with an established community affairs function, and the creation of a body which could represent the views of many different community bodies: these factors have evidently helped in improving lines of communication. There is a role for promotional and intermediary bodies such as BitC, which played a part in the establishment of the BSG for Moss Side, in acting as a broker between community groups and companies; however, there is no 'blueprint' for success in this activity, which needs sustained effort over a long period. Measures which could help in this area are:

* more personnel resources for intermediary bodies to involve themselves in a 'catalytic' way in localities and help form links between firms and the community;
* more provision of training courses for voluntary bodies on relationships with the private sector;
* more secondments of private sector personnel to voluntary bodies, and of staff from the latter into businesses, in order to promote mutual understanding and the transfer of skills and knowledge;
* better networking between community groups and intermediary organisations in order to provide businesses with good

'signposting' around the voluntary sector and develop common approaches to the private sector.

The role of local authorities

The missing element in a number of inner city initiatives involving business in recent years has been the participation of the local authority. In Manchester and Bristol political factors – in particular, resistance to the advent of the Urban Development Corporations – have led to less involvement by local authorities in local regeneration initiatives than many would like. Business respondents often stressed the need to bring local government into partnerships if full effectiveness was to be achieved. There are many signs that any initial hostility to business involvement and partnership with the private sector is fading, if not largely a thing of the past, in local authorities with inner city problems. In Birmingham the Heartlands initiative provides a striking example of collaboration between the private sector and a city council; in Bristol the local Business Leadership Team has begun work with the local authority as a member; in Sheffield there has been a much-reported sea-change in relations between the city council and the private sector, and partnership ventures have flourished (see Fogarty and Christie, 1991); in Manchester the local authority is represented on the Moss Side and Hulme Community Development Trust. Our business respondents certainly wanted to form partnerships with local authorities, and some were dismayed by what they saw as the marginalisation of councils in recent urban policy. Moves to bring local authorities whole-heartedly into partnership initiatives and cooperation with Urban Development Corporations are much to be encouraged.

Social regeneration in the inner city

There is a feeling among many community groups and also among a number of business respondents that *social regeneration* in inner city areas has been neglected in recent years by comparison with economic and infrastructural renewal. It is argued that partnership initiatives should bring in the voluntary sector to a greater extent in order to put social issues on the agenda or give them a higher priority. Moreover, there have been many criticisms of the pattern of urban renewal in the USA to the effect that it has been 'property-led' and has made little impact on the development of an urban underclass (see Carley, 1990;

Hambleton, 1990); similar criticisms of an emphasis on property development in inner city areas have been voiced in the UK (see Hambleton, 1990).

In many cases respondents from the private and public sector argued that wealth creation had to come first: without new infrastructure, companies would not invest in inner city areas; and without new investment and new businesses there would be no jobs for inner city residents. It is a strongly-held and well-articulated view, and clearly has force. However, even if it is accepted that major infrastructural 'flagship' initiatives and other economic investment measures should take precedence in urban renewal policy, it does not follow that all initiatives to tackle deep-seated social problems need to wait for property-led schemes to be completed. There is a widespread view that more could be done within the current framework to ensure that social issues receive due attention and resources. There are several pointers to positive ways of doing this.

First, it seems likely from our discussions with business leaders that funding cuts imposed on local authorities or central government initiatives – for example, in TEC funding – will not encourage allocation of more private sector resources; 'pump priming' funds will be necessary to attract more business resources into inner city ventures and disadvantaged areas.

Second, it was argued that the voluntary sector, which has considerable knowledge of local communities, needs to be brought into established partnership initiatives on a wider scale in order to help develop more effective projects. The voluntary sector already plays a part in the government's Urban Programme. In Bristol the Greater Bristol Trust, a community trust, is forming links with the local development corporation; in Manchester voluntary bodies have a voice in the committee structure of the local TEC; and as we have seen, Common Purpose is operating schemes for the formation of networks linking business leaders with community leaders among others. All of these developments seem worthy of extension. Development Corporations and TECs could form closer links with the lead community and voluntary sector bodies in their areas; Common Purpose, by bringing business and voluntary/public sector leaders together in city-wide training courses, promises much as a means of improving understanding of social problems by business leaders over the long term.

Third, numerous informants from all sectors felt that there was a general need for 'social regeneration' issues to be placed higher on the agendas of TECs, UDCs, Business Leadership Teams and equivalent strategic partnership bodies in the cities. It was acknowledged in our case study cities that there is scope for much more action by agencies incorporating local authority leaders and key business figures in areas of policy such as childcare facilities, homelessness, new housing and rehabilitation of existing housing, a major social problem in inner city areas.

Many of the obstacles mentioned above, and many of the possible ways of overcoming them, relate to the operation of networks and the coordination of initiatives. We examine problems in this area in the next section.

4.4 Improving information exchange and coordination

A constant refrain in our case studies was the complaint about the perceived lack of coherence of national and local initiatives and the inadequacy of information flows between key actors in community regeneration. Many recent studies confirm this as an area of frustration and confusion for businesses (see for example CBI, 1988; Fogarty and Christie, 1991; Segal Quince Wickstead, 1988). There are several dimensions to the problem:

- confusion over the multiplicity of government programmes in urban renewal;
- confusion over the fragmentation in many areas of the voluntary sector and community groups;
- confusion over the role of intermediary and promotional bodies;
- confusion over the plethora of partnership initiatives which have developed between business and the private sector in many cities and towns;
- a suspicion of widespread duplication of effort and subsequent cynicism over new ventures ('not another initiative!');
- a view that city-wide fora are needed to 'pull together' disparate initiatives and rationalise those which duplicate effort.

In this section we look at each of these in turn and propose a model for coordination of initiatives and information flows which draws on good practice in several localities. First, however, there is a key point to be made about the scope for reaching overall coherence in national and local initiatives. There is so much variation in local needs and circumstances that a grand national 'blueprint' is not feasible. Moreover, the multiplicity of issues to be tackled within the cities demands the involvement of a wide variety of bodies, which inevitably means that complex networks and information flows develop. Finally, as a number of respondents said, businesses need to be given a sense of 'ownership' of projects, and this tends to lead to the proliferation of schemes as companies seek to do their own thing as well as, or instead of, getting involved in partnerships. One respondent in Bristol said that 'if you are looking for coherence, you are spitting in the wind'; we do not go so far, but equally we do not feel that there is scope for a grand rationalisation of initiatives.

The potential for confusion over public sector programmes and for lack of coordination between government programmes was often mentioned by respondents, and has been commented upon in a recent report of the House of Commons Public Accounts Committee (Committee of Public Accounts, 1990) and in a report by the Audit Commission on urban regeneration (Audit Commission, 1989). There is clearly a widespread view that improved communications are called for between the different departments of state involved in the Action for Cities programme, and that the various component programmes should be simplified.

Fragmentation of the voluntary sector and of community groups is a problem in many areas. Wholesale rationalisation is neither feasible nor desirable, since there is healthy competition in this sector as in others and, in any case, groups are formed in response to strongly felt needs and problems and few would consider themselves to be duplicating someone else's work. However, there is scope for selective mergers in the interest of groups themselves in a climate of increasing competition for resources; and there is scope for the formation of more effective umbrella groups and community trusts which can represent voluntary sector and community views to businesses and others, and which can act as a contact point for them.

The main national intermediary bodies have come together in the 'Bridge Group' to improve information exchange between themselves and coordination of activities. This type of coordination could usefully be mirrored at regional and local level among the intermediaries. For this to happen, the intermediaries need more resources for staffing and for marketing in order to make themselves better known to the business world beyond the established corporate contributors to the community. There are also specific problems for Business in the Community, the main national promotional body. Our respondents echoed the view of many reported in Fogarty and Christie (1991) that BitC has spread itself too thinly and set up too many initiatives which have often been inadequately followed up; and that it is not well equipped to deliver projects in its own right. There is a widely-held view that BitC should concentrate its resources on what it can do most effectively, namely promoting the cause of community investment and acting as a catalyst for action in localities, bringing companies into play and involving appropriate specialist agencies in project delivery.

The development of many public programmes and of initiatives for inter-firm and multi-sector partnership in recent years has inevitably led to confusion and suspicions of duplication. In all three of our case study cities respondents expressed frustration and dismay at what they saw as a chaotic proliferation of ventures and acronyms, about which they felt ill-informed and confused. As the Audit Commission has remarked in relation to urban policy, '...it is hard to escape the conclusion that at the level of the individual city there can be programme overkill with a strategic vacuum' (Audit Commission, 1989, p.32). This is a serious problem for partnerships, and could be a deterrent to some companies to get involved in community ventures. There is also a problem for participants in various initiatives in obtaining up-to-date information about what others are doing. What solutions might there be to this problem which do not involve unrealistic attempts at rationalisation according to an inflexible blueprint?

Coordinating partnerships and improving information exchange: ideas for discussion

At national level, the formation of the Bridge Group of agencies is a positive move in improving communication and coordination between promotional and intermediary organisations. There could be merit in widening the group into a 'Community Investment Forum', which would also bring in, on perhaps a quarterly basis, representatives of lead national business bodies such as the CBI; the National Training Task Force; and the government departments involved in the various inner cities programmes. Such a forum could also contribute to improved communication between government departments on inner city initiatives.

At the local level, there are two areas which need to be considered. First, strategic fora for coordination of partnership activities and information exchange about initiatives at a city-wide level (or at an equivalent level in rural areas); second, the development of networks at the operational level linking companies with community groups and other actors.

Local Community Investment Fora
The key requirement, according to respondents in many organisations, is for an overall 'lead' strategic 'Community Investment Forum' within cities for coordination of partnership initiatives. This would ensure that schemes do not proliferate unduly, and would provide a focus for enquiries from, and information provision to, organisations in all sectors. This body needs to include representatives of, or at least have excellent contacts with, the private sector, local authority, urban development corporation (if one exists), voluntary sector representation, and bodies from intermediary agencies. It would become the lead body in localities for various functions in relation to business action in the community. For example:

- lead role in coordinating the flow of information around local networks of companies and public/voluntary sector bodies in relation to business action in communities;
- forum for discussion and action on community investment issues and on multi-sector partnerships in infrastructural development and social regeneration;
- close liaison with Business Leadership Teams and equivalent partnership bodies;
- partnership with BitC in establishing new local Per Cent Clubs;
- partnership with Common Purpose in setting up new Common Purpose initiatives.

Which bodies would join such a forum would depend on the circumstances in each area. It would comprise representatives of the local authority, leading firms and business-led groups such as Business Leadership Teams (where they exist), the Chamber of Commerce, the TEC or LEC, educational institutions, the urban development corporation where one exists, City Action Team and Task Force where these exist, and leading local voluntary agencies and umbrella groups.

There is a mixed pattern in our case study cities in relation to overall fora for partnership initiatives. The new Bristol BLT, the

Bristol Initiative, seems to have overcome any problems in fitting into the existing network of business-led organisations and formed a strong link with the TEC, and to have filled the gap for a city-wide strategic forum. In Birmingham the Heartlands Initiative is the nearest equivalent to what is being proposed: however, there is clearly a demand in the city for a distinct coordinating forum, and the key Heartlands partners, the City Council and Chamber of Commerce, could, in collaboration with local TECs, develop one. In Manchester the TEC and the North West BLT share numerous members, but the BLT appears to be seen by many as 'remote' and 'mysterious': it may be that its regional coverage is too broad, and that a distinct Manchester forum is needed to complement the TEC.

The use of an existing body to act as the strategic coordinating forum and 'signposting' body in relation to partnership ventures is desirable: there are already more initiatives than many companies and other bodies can keep track of, and yet another wholly new organisation in a crowded field would be superfluous. However, the type of body most appropriate to the task of acting as the hub of a network and as lead body for a coordinating forum will vary from city to city.

It is likely that the TECs and LECs in many areas have the potential to take on the role of the nodal point in local networks of agencies involved in community investment; and that the TEC area could be used more generally as a unit for new initiatives involving companies in community action. There are a number of factors which could favour this:

- their remit embraces many aspects of community investment: for instance, enterprise promotion, targeted recruitment and training initiatives, and education/industry links;
- the TECs and LECs form a ready-made network for other bodies to use and fit into;
- they have succeeded in attracting the support of many companies which may be expected to be involved in or to wish to get involved in community investment initiatives;
- they cover a manageable local area;
- many are already well-known to businesses and the voluntary sector and could therefore be a good focus for referring enquiries from either sector to the other, and as a source of referrals to other bodies in their area.

One objection which might be raised to this suggestion is that the TECs and LECs have a very heavy workload in training and enterprise development and are unlikely to be able to address broader infrastructural and social problems for a considerable time. They are also subject to constraints on financial and staffing resources which make it difficult for them to embrace wider issues of community investment. Moreover, the TEC/LEC network is still being established and the development of a leading role in promoting and coordinating partnership ventures between different sectors must be seen as something that a number of TECs and LECs might wish to move towards over several years.

Thus, while many TECs and LECs might wish to develop a role in setting up a strategic forum and acting as a focal point for information flows on community investment and partnership initiatives, other bodies might be more appropriate in other areas. The lead could be taken by a Chamber of Commerce, a Business Leadership Team, by one or more leading employers, or by a private/ public sector forum such as Sheffield's Economic Regeneration Committee, based in the City Council.

What is crucial is that such a local strategic forum should be attached to an existing body that is well-known to business, which has good relations and contacts with representative bodies in all sectors in the local community, and which can fund and facilitate mechanisms for coordination of partnership initiatives and information exchange.

In order to improve the exchange of information and referral of enquiries it would be advantageous for any new ventures related to community investment by business to become affiliated to local fora. For instance, any new local Per Cent Clubs or Common Purpose initiatives, along with other bodies such as enterprise agencies and community trusts, could become 'affiliated' to the local Community Investment Forum. This form of association should help to improve information flows and provide a focus for enquiries and referrals from companies and community bodies in relation to business support for the community. Each Forum, working with relevant local partners, could develop local directories, to be updated annually, of organisations in all sectors involved in community action of different kinds. This kind of activity would also provide affiliated bodies with the information needed to play a more effective role in referring enquiries to other parts of the local network of agencies involved in community action. As noted by Segal, Quince, Wickstead (1988), truly effective networking implies the capacity of all support organisations to carry out a 'signposting' referral function to some degree, even where there is an acknowledged lead body.

Obviously this proposal implies new work for Chambers of Commerce, TECs or other bodies in housing a local forum and acting as a key 'signposting' centre, and in helping to establish affiliate membership for local Per Cent Clubs and new ventures such as Common Purpose. It is clear that in many cases more resources and considerable training would be needed for this to happen. However, this proposed pattern could bring greater coherence to local partnerships and promotion of business links with the community, and would simplify and improve information flows and referral mechanisms. At the same time it is not a rigid blueprint, and provides for the broad basis for cooperation only.

Coordination at grassroots level
At the grassroots operational level there are already local employer networks and TEC sub-groups which are delivering training and enterprise projects and programmes and acting as information networks. These could be complemented by an extension to other localities of two developments which we have come across.

First, the development of local networks, linked to each local Community Investment Forum, of 'funding fora' as have been established in Bristol and Sheffield to promote information exchange between companies, local council grant providers, business groups and voluntary sector umbrella groups and community trusts on funding of local community projects and charities. As with the strategic level, networking of this kind would equip all relevant organisations with the information needed to act as a signposting/referral body to some extent.

Second, the establishment, for Task Force areas and other 'problem' localities, of Business Support Groups and Community Development Trusts on the Moss Side and Hulme model.

Taken together, these recommendations lead to a model for coordination and information flows in localities at a strategic and operational level as shown below. We hope that this proposal will receive further discussion and elaboration as a means, not of imposing a rigid framework on widely differing areas, but of establishing a general pattern for networking which will simplify coordination of initiatives and make information exchange and 'signposting' much easier than it currently is.

Local networks centred on a Community Investment Forum

Based in (eg):
- Chamber of Commerce
- TEC/LEC
- local authority

Strategic city-wide level

Local Community Investment Forum

Members from (eg):
- Chamber of Commerce
- TEC/LEC
- Local Authority
- Higher education
- Voluntary sector
- Local employers
- CATs/Task Forces
- UDC

Affiliated bodies (eg):
- Per Cent Club
- Business Support Groups
- Enterprise Agencies
- Local employer networks

Operational/ district level bodies

Of course, improvements to organisational patterns as suggested above are only part of what is needed to overcome the obstacles which our informants have identified. In order to make a real difference to the community investment scene, they need to accompany other measures of the kind outlined in this section.

5 Summary of Key Messages for Managers and Policy Makers

- Community investment on the part of the private sector has developed considerably in the last ten years. There are many successes on which to build, and there is scope for companies of all sizes and sectors to become active in different forms of community support. Although charitable donations remain an important aspect of business support for the community, many companies increasingly lay emphasis on forms of involvement such as secondments, school-industry links, and training and local recruitment. The growing importance of these forms of support reflect a movement among companies and intermediary bodies to promote community action as a form of business *investment*, which merits integration with mainstream business activities. There has been, then, a move away from the concept of *charitable giving* towards that of *community investment.*
- Companies become involved in forms of community investment not only from a sense of corporate social responsibility, but also out of enlightened self-interest. Companies and promotional bodies increasingly recognise that there are potential short- and long-term benefits to business from community investment. These relate to goodwill in the community, positive publicity, employee relations, relations with shareholders and customers, recruitment opportunities, partnership with other organisations, and long-term social stability and economic prosperity .
- Companies are involved in direct links with community bodies; in inter-firm partnerships; and in multi-sector partnerships involving

public agencies, local authorities and the voluntary sector. The partnership approach is often crucial to the success of initiatives to tackle complex inner city problems, and is a key area for encouragement of more company activity.

- Good practice in community investment is associated with clear corporate policies which specify areas of priority for support, identify areas of company expertise which can be brought to bear, secure company-wide commitment to action, give long-term backing from the board, and provide for flexibility in meeting local needs.

- There are substantial challenges for the 1990s in consolidating and extending the culture of community investment by business. Momentum needs to be sustained in the face of economic recession, many more companies need to be recruited, and policy development by companies of all sizes needs to be improved, especially among small and medium-sized companies.

- Measures which are likely to help meet these challenges include:
  - dissemination of guidelines for good practice by companies in organisation and policy development for community involvement;
  - more resources for marketing and consultancy by intermediary and promotional agencies to companies, especially to small and medium companies;
  - further development of initiatives such as Common Purpose for bringing business leaders into networks with decision makers from the public and voluntary sector;
  - establishment of more local Per Cent Clubs around the country;
  - development of more management courses in corporate social responsibility in business schools around the country;
  - establishment of improved systems for training community affairs managers within businesses;
  - action by committed businesses to encourage suppliers and corporate customers to become more involved in community investment;
  - long-term commitment to partnership initiatives by government agencies and businesses in the inner cities, with the involvement of local authorities and community bodies;

– use of broad-based local 'Community Investment Fora' involving business (such as the local TECs and LECs) as a focus for networks of partnership initiatives in cities and other localities and for improved coordination of projects and information between companies, public bodies and other community organisations.

Part II

Case Studies of Three Cities

6 Introduction to the City Case Studies

A programme of case study interviews was carried out in Birmingham, Bristol and Manchester. Initial meetings with the government's City Action Teams and Task Forces were used to identify companies considered to be active in community initiatives and potential examples of good practice, and public and voluntary agencies with a perspective on company investment in the community.

The aims of the city case studies were: to obtain an overview of business activity in the community on a city-wide scale, although with a particular focus on inner city areas in which the government's Task Forces were active; to highlight examples of good practice among companies and initiatives in which business played a key role; and to identify constraints on good practice by the private sector.

In a short study of this kind the picture obtained of activity in the cities cannot be claimed to be comprehensive. We have deliberately focussed on instances of business activity which potentially offer good practice lessons, and of course there is no suggestion that these are typical of most companies in the case study cities. Moreover, there be no question of being able to supply a full evaluation of any of the initiatives which are being developed. However, we hope that the case studies will provide useful overviews of the range of activity to be found in the cities visited, and helpful illustrations of the role being played by numerous businesses.

The different situations in each city are reflected in the case studies. The Birmingham study contains a detailed account of the infrastructural initiatives launched there, which have dominated business involvement in community investment to date. In Bristol the emphasis is more on the pattern of company links with the voluntary sector, the development of policies for community involvement, and the relationship of public and voluntary bodies to the private sector. In Manchester the focus is on economic development in the inner city areas and the attempt to bring them into contact with new opportunities for enterprise and employment.

Each city case study is organised in the same way. An introductory overview of recent economic developments and of the main actors in community initiatives is followed by an examination of company links with the community and a review of various partnership ventures involving business, and then a review of constraints on good practice identified by respondents. Each section concludes with selected detailed case studies of companies or business partnership initiatives.

7 Case Study: Birmingham

7.1 Introduction

Birmingham provides an interesting case study of the activities of the private sector in urban regeneration for two reasons. First, there is an almost bewildering number of initiatives which have some private sector involvement. Second, arguably Birmingham is posed to replicate, in the near future, Glasgow's urban regeneration success. That this is possible is due to the sheer number of initiatives, now reaching a threshold of 'synergistic' activity; to the broad scope of the initiatives addressing the complex issues of urban renewal; a long history of pragmatic partnerships that exist between the private sector and local government in Birmingham; and to a long-term, strategic perspective shared between the alternating Labour and Conservative controlled local councils. These conclusions are substantiated by recent analysis of urban regeneration in Glasgow (Carley, 1990).

Recognition that Birmingham is in such a favoured position does not mean downplaying the enormity of the task remaining, nor the difficult position of the city in the early 1980s. Birmingham, as a major city in the industrial heartland of Britain, suffered substantially from the effects of deindustrialisation and from recession. Many firms went out of business; others, such as the then British Leyland, shed half their staff or more in an effort to remain competitive. In the period between 1979 and 1981 incomes per head in the West Midlands plummeted from being second only to the South East to being the lowest in Britain. A wave of redundancies meant that in 1979 and 1980 alone one quarter of a million jobs were lost, manufacturing output decreased by one quarter, and unemployment trebled.

In addition, the penchant in the 1960s for large-scale urban clearance and reconstruction had left a dramatic mark on Birmingham: a city centre encircled by motorways and bearing witness to many of the design mistakes of the period, and one of the largest house clearance programmes in the country in the immediate inner ring around the city centre, an area now comprising high and low rise council estates, some remaining industry and much derelict industrial land. Generally Birmingham, like Glasgow, not only had many serious problems, but it also had a poor reputation to overcome.

However the seeds of Birmingham's urban regeneration success were already germinating in the early 1980s, sown by one partnership after another between the City of Birmingham and the private sector. One exercise in partnership, the National Exhibition Centre (NEC), goes back to the late 1960s when the local authority teamed up with the Birmingham Chamber of Industry and Commerce to attract this important national facility to Birmingham. The NEC Ltd. was established in 1970, with the City Council and the Chamber as equal partners. This successful (and now profitable) arrangement continues. As Sir Robert Booth, Director of the Chamber at the time and past Chairman of NEC Ltd. notes:

> In retrospect it was an historic occasion. It led to a unique partnership
> of civic and private enterprise, with bi-partisan support given by the
> Conservative and Labour leaders.

This tradition of municipal action, partnership, and major flagship projects continues to underpin the local authority's strategy to promote Birmingham as a centre for financial and service industries, and as centre for leisure and tourism.

Central to that strategy is the new International Convention Centre (ICC), set for completion in April 1991, and developed and managed by NEC. In addition to creating about 2000 jobs and generating spending of about £50 million in the first year, the ICC is a major pump priming exercise in attracting private sector investment into the city, including for example a new £34 million, five star Hyatt Hotel. The ICC development also includes the National Indoor Arena for sporting events and new venue for the acclaimed City of Birmingham Symphony Orchestra. Birmingham's efforts at cultural regeneration are also apparent from the recent shift from London of both the Sadler's Wells dance company (now Birmingham Royal Ballet) and the D'Oyly Carte Opera Company to the city.

In addition to direct benefits, the ICC promises to be a further inducement to an initiative of the City Council and the government's local City Action Team (CAT) to refurbish the city centre generally, called the Highbury Initiative (see section 7.3 below). Although much has been done in the way of environmental improvement, there are major plans within the context of this initiative to tear down the 1960s Bull Ring shopping development and replace it with something more user- and pedestrian-friendly, and to bridge the motorway ring road wherever possible with pedestrian areas.

All this activity is indicative of a major resurgence in the economy of Birmingham, in particular a dramatic growth in the service sector. Between 1980 and 1987 some 17,000 new firms were created, with substantial growth in the service and financial sectors and some more limited recovery in a reduced manufacturing sector.

Inner city issues

Clearly this amount of urban regeneration could not occur without substantial activity by the private sector as well as on the part of the local authority. However, it is also necessary to question whether the benefits of this volume of private and public investment and other activity extend to the residents of the inner city of Birmingham as well as the city at large. This important question is hardly a foregone conclusion. For example a recent study of urban renewal, reviewing American efforts at regeneration, noted that inner city residents in US cities were left out of developments and often further marginalised by city centre regeneration (Carley, 1990). It was not possible to answer the question within the confines of the short study reported here, but a necessary beginning has been made in highlighting promising and successful ventures and constraints on good practice.

The focus of this case study is on activities in which the private sector has played a part in the inner city of Birmingham, the 'doughnut' as it were around the city centre. This inner city area consists of industrial land, both occupied and derelict, council estates, and just outside the ring of council estates, Victorian neighbourhoods of mainly two storey, terraced housing. These neighbourhoods are now the lively home of many of Birmingham's ethnic minority residents, for example, Afro-Caribbeans in Handsworth and Sparkbrook, and Asians such as Gujaratis, Punjabis and Bangladeshis in Saltley and Sparkbrook.

Birmingham has the largest ethnic minority population of any district authority in the country, about 150,000 residents from the New Commonwealth, accounting for 15 per cent of the population of the City as a whole, and 43 per cent of the population of the inner city. Overcrowding in housing of ethnic minority residents is a serious problem – 47 per cent of families are overcrowded compared with just 2 per cent of white families. Many ethnic minority residents, particularly Asians, are in business, and of these 80 per cent are in the retail sector and 20 per cent in manufacturing.

It was decided to focus the limited time available in the study to examining private sector involvement in the regeneration of East Birmingham, including the mainly Asian neighbourhood of Saltley, and other initiatives which had mainly an inner city content. In this we benefited from the helpful advice of the City Action Team and the East Birmingham Task Force, which superseded the previous Task Force in Handsworth.

This is therefore an overview of private sector and major public-private partnership initiatives, but it has not been possible to analyse the effectiveness of the contribution of individual firms nor the overall impact of initiatives. Moreover, there are of course many other community initiatives involving public, voluntary and private sector support in the city which we have not been able to include in this account. The research has however resulted in a general model of private sector involvement in urban regeneration, many examples of good practice, and some information on constraints on that good practice.

7.2 Companies and their community links

The contributions of private sector firms to urban regeneration in Birmingham are many and varied. For this reason it was found helpful to devise a framework for understanding these contributions; this was derived from a review of the material generated during the course of interviews with participants and recipients of urban regeneration activities. Like any framework, it is a simplification and there are exceptions, nevertheless it encompasses most of the private sector activities in Birmingham.

We also make use of this general framework in the case studies of Bristol and Manchester below.

Three levels of activity can be identified:
* Level one: direct links between firms and the community
* Level two: multi-firm groupings to address urban regeneration issues
* Level three: partnerships between private, public and/or voluntary sectors

The levels are not mutually exclusive, on the contrary many, mostly larger, firms are involved in all three levels of activity. The benefits to urban regeneration to flow from activity at more than one level is probably more than additive; the complex, multi-sector nature of the task of urban regeneration suggests that multi-firm groupings and partnerships are both necessary and provide 'symbiotic' benefits as a result of the interaction (Carley, 1990). As such, levels two and three are valuable complements to activities of the firm at level one.

The remainder of this chapter describes the activities of private sector firms in Birmingham in terms of the model, highlights the good practice of some firms, and draws some general conclusions about constraints on the development of good practice in business involvement.

Direct links between companies and the community
The case studies highlighted four areas of activity by firms in Birmingham which are making a particular contribution to urban regeneration and to quality of life in the inner city. These are:
* employment training and youth training, pre-training activities such as basic skills enhancement, basic literacy and numeracy, and English as a second language (ESL) courses for people from ethnic minority groups;
* small business promotion and counselling for prospective entrepreneurs in the inner city;
* building refurbishment in hitherto derelict inner city areas, usually rather than expansion on green field sites;
* urban renewal initiatives involving the reclamation of derelict industrial land into new business or science parks.

Training
There is substantial involvement of firms in the direct provision of training in Birmingham, too much to describe in total. One obvious area is the provision of Youth Training, mainly for 16 to 17 year olds,

leading towards job-related qualifications, usually a National Vocational Qualification (NVQ). In the private sector this is usually based on on-the-job training. In Birmingham more than 70 national and local firms offer youth training, and more are involved through their respective industrial training associations, for example, the Construction Industry Training Board.

Fewer firms are involved in Employment Training for 18-59-year old unemployed for more than six months. The Training Agency (1989) lists a number of firms including Comet Group, Dixons, the Football League, Habitat, Herons Service Stations, Mothercare, and the Wimpey Group from among the dozen or so to participate in ET. But many other firms offer their own, often sophisticated, training programmes to suit their needs. For example, the Birmingham-headquartered multinational IMI, whose activities are described in detail in a separate case study in section 7.5 below, offers post-graduate engineering and management training as well as craft and technician apprenticeships and clerical training for 16 and 17 year olds.

Another large firm with a substantial commitment to training is the Rover Group, who are among a number of firms to make a determined, quantified effort to increase the proportion of applications for trainee posts from inner city residents and people from ethnic minority communities. These efforts are described in the section below on multi-firm groups and in a separate case study.

Grand Metropolitan Community Services (GMCS) is involved in support for training initiatives via its local training agency BACTA, which delivers courses in partnership with the East Birmingham Task Force. BACTA is also involved in support for the local GATE initiative (Group for Action in Training and Employment), which seeks to link job seekers from the local ethnic minority communities with job opportunities with major employers in Birmingham which have skill shortages and find it hard to recruit from the ethnic groups.

Smaller firms also participate in training initiatives. Two Saltley-based firms were interviewed for the research. One, a small industrial firm in Saltley since 1985, specialises in training young Asian women to work fairly complex, imported industrial machinery, of a type for which there is no other hands-on training in Birmingham. Apart from the benefits to the community of its location directly in an inner city, largely ethnic minority neighbourhood, the firm has taken careful steps to arrange its hiring, training, and work practices to be acceptable to the local Muslim population, with assistance from a Muslim community group.

Another firm, an up and coming video production and duplicating company in Saltley, also offers training on sophisticated equipment, in this case a 'high band' video editing studio and broadcast specification camera equipment. The training initiative was prompted by the local Task Force, which brought the company together with Birmingham Heartlands, and provided some part funding. The location of the firm in the inner city, and its connections with community groups, means that a high proportion of its trainees are from local ethnic minority backgrounds. The trainees benefit from hands-on experience of sophisticated equipment; the firm benefits, in our informant's words, from:

> the chance to give something back to the community and from finding useful, reliable people who are few and far between.

There are of course constraints on private sector involvement in training, discussed later. In terms of the larger issue of economic regeneration, it is impossible for a small study to assess the effectiveness of observed private sector involvement, or more importantly, whether the magnitude of the training on offer is anywhere near sufficient for the needs of the community.

Small business promotion
The growth of new businesses is an important aspect of urban regeneration. These replace industrial firms gone out of business or contracted in size, they provide local employment, and they bring money into local communities and generate multiplier effects. In Birmingham new small businesses are nurtured by a number of enterprise agencies, for example Just for Starters in Saltley, funded in part by the East Birmingham Task Force. Other group efforts include that of the Institute of Asian Businesses, linked to the Chamber of Commerce, and Black Business in Birmingham (3B), funded in part by the Home Office, the CAT and the City Council. Other neighbourhoods in Birmingham have their counterpart to Just for Starters.

The National Westminister Bank in Birmingham is active in providing assistance to prospective entrepreneurs in inner city neighbourhoods. This is part of a broader commitment to local communities, which is reflected in the company policy that one per cent of bottom line profits should go back into the community. The underlying assumption is one of enlightened self-interest:

> ...if the local community is thriving the bank must benefit through savings and lending.

Although Natwest's community policy goes back a decade, it was the inner city disturbances of 1984-85 which prompted a new focus on the specific problems of the inner city districts. In Birmingham this focus was naturally on racially-troubled area of Handsworth, but the company's activity has now broadened across the inner city. Natwest's direct involvement is threefold. First, a Natwest manager has been seconded to the important regeneration intiative Birmingham Heartlands, described below, as its commercial manager. Second, there is a secondee from Natwest to the Women's Enterprise Development Agency. Third, Natwest has designated a Business Development Manager (BDM) to work directly in inner city areas and on urban regeneration tasks in Birmingham. These three people are among 27 Natwest staff nationwide seconded to urban regeneration tasks. Six of these are Business Development Managers for inner city areas.

In terms of the work of the BDM for Birmingham, Natwest's corporate expectation is of the possibility of profits in the long term, but there are no targets associated with this work and there is, as the BDM says, 'lots of freedom to get involved in the inner city'. The BDM's remit is threefold. First, he offers free business start-up advice, in the community, and in sessions 'not the usual one-half an hour, but for 3-4 hours at a go if necessary, and at 8 o'clock at night in block of council flats if required'. This advice may include financial packaging of bank funds, grant aid, soft loans and Task Force monies as required. Here simply knowing what is available is helpful to the entrepreneur. Regular counselling sessions are also offered at agencies such as Just for Starters. Second, the BDM offers financial expertise to voluntary organisations active in the inner city, for example, to the Handsworth Employment Scheme. Finally, the BDM has an education and community liaison role, speaking in schools and at Enterprise Agencies, and working with the CAT, the Task Force, the TEC and with the Enterprise Allowance Scheme.

The BDM scheme would seem to merit close study by other cities and by other companies with expertise to offer. It provides a flexible form of support to inner city areas and draws on the company's core skills and knowledge to make a well focussed contribution to local activity.

Inner city building refurbishment
Turning from human resource development to bricks and mortar, some companies in Birmingham have recognised that the inner city offers the possibility of the imaginative renovation of derelict buildings into business premises. One company which has relocated to a renovated building in the inner city is Bucknall Austin, a quantity surveying and project management practice, with 17 offices in Britain and elsewhere in Europe. In 1985, having outgrown its premises, it decided to look for a property suitable for refurbishment and settled on a derelict Victorian glass factory. The building had been empty for seven years and was in a very derelict state, with only the external walls sound. Nevertheless, the partners decided to pass up safer options, and to gamble on a canalside location in an area ripe for entry by business. The chairman of the firm is quoted in *Business West Midlands*:

> With the current trend in green issues, I would like to see more companies take a creative stance and consider renovation of older properties as a viable alternative to green field sites.

Urban renewal initiatives
Very few individual firms are directly involved in the regeneration of derelict inner city areas on their own. As might be expected, this typically involves some partnership effort, for example, partnerships between the City of Birmingham and private firms in Birmingham Heartlands or in the development of the Aston Science Park. These partnerships are discussed in section 7.3 below.

One firm that has undertaken what is virtually its own urban renewal programme is the multinational IMI, probably the largest company headquartered in Birmingham. On 110 acres of their own surplus industrial land they have created a landscaped business park and an ecological reserve in the inner city, adjacent to the Heartlands development area. This interesting long-term project is described in the separate company case study in section 7.5.

7.3 Partnerships and networks
Multi-firm partnerships for community action
In a number of innovative ways firms in Birmingham have joined together to tackle the complex challenges of urban regeneration. Three are described here.

Birmingham Chamber of Industry and Commerce
Birmingham is fortunate in having what has been described as 'one of the most active Chambers of Commerce in the country'.

An examination of its activities with an urban regeneration focus, on behalf of its 4,400 members, bears out this contention, and suggests that, with the Local Authority, the Chamber is a major force in regeneration in Birmingham. In the space available here it is only possible to outline some of its work. In addition to its pivotal role in the NEC and Heartlands, and management role in the new Convention Centre, the Chamber:

- has established Local Employer Networks (LENs) which link education and training establishments with manufacturing and service industries, on a 12-sector basis, to match training provision with employers' needs. LENs are providing a basis for organisation of the grassroots operations of the new Birmingham TEC;
- has established its own 'community programme' to provide employment for the skilled and unskilled long-term unemployed, for example landscape refurbishment in association with Cadburys;
- through Birmingham Chamber Training Ltd, provides work experience and training for young people (325 places) and the unemployed (275 places);
- houses an enterprise agency, Birmingham Venture, which provides assistance to new entrepreneurs. This is funded 100 per cent by private firms, relying on them for donations and secondments;
- is working with Inner City Partnership to establish an Industrial Crime Watch scheme similar to Neighbourhood Watch;
- has established the Institute of Asian Business, with pump-priming funds from the City Action Team, to encourage Birmingham's more than 4000 Asian businesses to become more involved in the

development of the local economy, local employment, training, and to do more in the way of charitable giving.

The Chamber has also been instrumental in the establishment of Birmingham's first Schools Compact, in conjunction with Birmingham Heartlands. This has now broadened into a formal Education – Business Partnership in which a task group of 20 key employers under Sir Adrian Cadbury is linked to 500 schools through the Local Education Authority. The Chamber is also the contract holder with the Department of Trade and Industry for providing advisers who assess suitability of firms for participation in Compact, for work experience placement, and for two-week teacher placements in companies.

Birmingham Business Action Team
The Business Action Team (BAT) has a highly distinctive niche in the spectrum of urban regeneration efforts – their focus is on assisting inner city firms with up to 200 employees in imminent danger of going out of business, thus resulting in a loss of employment and local income. The idea originated in one of the city's business entreprise centres, and initial three year funding has been provided by the CAT. The Business Action Team in turn makes use of management and financial expertise from mid-career secondees from private firms, which have included British Telecom, Cadburys, British Gas, Ansells, Glynwed, Foseco, Tarmac, Streetley and British Rail.

BAT reckons that it has saved more than 350 inner city jobs, at a cost considerably less than the going rate for job creation by public funding. Its three years of public funding concludes in 1990-91 and the BAT is intended to become a self-funded company, in essence a non-profit management consultancy. In the absence of sufficient funds from the private sector, BAT will have to start charging some, mainly non-inner city, clients commercial rates. There is concern that this will dilute both its inner city focus and its charitable orientation.

The BAT is a venture which deserves study by other cities, given the vulnerability of many start-up firms in the inner city districts and the urgent need for follow-up support once small firms have been established with the help of enterprise agencies and public bodies such as the Task Forces. The BAT provides a model which City Action Teams and Task Forces elsewhere could use in putting together plans for private sector involvement in their districts.

The Ten Company Group Equal Opportunity Project
A major multi-firm initiative is the Ten Company Group Equal
Opportunity Project. This began in 1988 when research by the
Training Agency revealed that, although 17 per cent of Birmingham's
school leavers are from ethnic minority backgrounds, only an average
of 4 per cent were being recruited as trainees by major firms. Ten of
these firms decided to band together to alter the situation, by a series
of regular, monthly meetings to review progress and good practice.
The companies are the Rover Group, Bromwich Catering, Central
Midland Co-operative Society, Construction Industry Training Board,
Hardy Spicer, Land Rover, Lucas Industries, Nigel Carter, Sainsbury's
and TSB Bank. These original ten members were joined by a further
twelve firms in 1989 and by ten more in 1990.

Two project workers were hired, with funding for salaries from
the City Action Team and for interim salary costs and overheads by
the Rover Group, to act as facilitators, do research, and to assist with
ethnic monitoring in firms and advise on possible changes in company
policy. In addition the companies themselves committed substantial
staff time of their representatives to the workings of the group.

The main aims of the Ten Company Group are:
• helping member companies identify and implement good equal
  opportunities practices;
• disseminating these good practices to other training providers;
• establishing links with ethnic minority communities in
  Birmingham, and with schools and other employer-led training
  schemes;
• providing for continuity of emphasis on equal opportunities
  amongst employers.

The companies involved in the original project are still active and
continue to work together; funding from the CAT and the TEC for a
project worker was agreed in early 1991 for a further year. Through
this project worker the Group's initiatives will be disseminated via the
TEC's emerging sector compacts. As noted above, two more groups
of companies, attracted by good publicity of the initiative, formed in
1989 and 1990. Between them they have a substantial proportion of
the Youth Trainees and of the employed status trainees in the city.

The record of success of the Groups is notable. The number and
proportion of trainees from ethnic minority backgrounds has trebled

among the original Group and doubled for the new companies who linked up in 1989. As one company representative noted:

> Equal opportunity policy isn't altruistic, its just good business sense. Without it we'd be missing out on mountains of talent in Birmingham's ethnic communities.

The Group has also established new links with schools and non-employer led training schemes. Three excellent publications have been developed:

- *Saying Yes*, a guide to good practice written for employers;
- *Working Together*, practical cases studies of the efforts of companies;
- *Action Handbook*, a directory of company and non-employer led training schemes for Birmingham.

All these were formally launched, with high profile media coverage, at appropriate locations such as the Handsworth Employment Scheme (a major inner city training centre), and a number of national presentations have been made. As many as 5000 copies of *Saying Yes* have been distributed to firms and agencies in Birmingham's inner city. This widespread publicity on equal opportunity good practice has generated enough interest locally for a third group to form, and similar groups are also being established in other cities in England based on this model. The initiative clearly has made a valuable contribution and its lead is being followed up elsewhere. The development of locally focussed handbooks as listed above is especially useful and worth emulation by similar initiatives in other cities in order to improve information exchange.

Multi-sector partnerships for community regeneration
Efforts to contribute to urban regeneration by firms and groups of firms in Birmingham are complemented by partnerships which link the private sector with central and local government and with voluntary organisations. There are a number of good examples.

Birmingham Heartlands
Birmingham Heartlands is a substantial, long-term urban regeneration partnership of Birmingham City Council, the Birmingham Chamber of Industry and Commerce, and five major development companies: Bryants, R M Douglas, Gallifords, Tarmac and Wimpey. The former

three are Birmingham-based, while the latter two are national companies. The partners have formed themselves into an non-statutory urban development agency which is probably unique in scale and organisation in the UK.

The Heartlands area begins just to the east of the city centre and covers 2,350 acres, including the Spaghetti Junction motorway intersection on the M6. In the area there are 650 existing companies, mostly small and medium-sized enterprises but also including such well-known names as DAF/Freight Rover, Jaguar, Rover Group and Metro-Cammell. There are also 12,900 residents of Heartlands, 81 per cent of whom are tenants of the local authority. More than 32 per cent of the residents are unemployed.

At the start of the Heartlands initiative the area was characterised by classic features of decline and decay:

- a declining economy attributable to traditional firms closing or contracting;
- more than 700 acres of derelict land, much of it consisting of contaminated ground or that with heavy foundations intact, and in scattered pockets unsuitable for assembly;
- a severe concentration of social and economic deprivation in the resident population, with Nechells ward among the most deprived 10 per cent in the country; and
- inadequate investment in the economic, physical and social assets of the area in spite of a number of public sector programmes aimed at regeneration.

In 1987, mindful of the scale of the problem and that its already stretched housing investment programme alone could not turn the area around, and of the prospect of the imposition of a statutory central government-controlled Urban Development Corporation for the area, Birmingham City Council began putting out feelers to the private sector about creating a partnership. The Chamber of Commerce offered to act as a go-between to local development companies, and subsequently to the big national partners of Wimpey and Tarmac.

The first task of the fledgling partnership was to commission a report by Roger Tym and Partners, which reviewed the existing constraints and potential for development, and proposed an overall strategy for this area of East Birmingham. The study was paid for jointly by the City Council, the developers and the Department of the Environment. The study argued that a piecemeal approach was flawed by a lack of overall strategy and that a 'radical restructuring' was required. Following three months of public consultation by the City Council, this gave rise to an East Birmingham strategy and the Heartlands Partnership.

The Partnership is led by Birmingham Heartlands Limited (BHL), a private sector company, 65 per cent of which is owned by the five developers and 35 per cent of which is owned by the City Council. The aims of the company are to provide a strategic framework which coordinates activity within Heartlands, to market and promote the area, to aid the assembly of land and development packages, to promote new development projects, and to support training and community development efforts. The City Council in turn retains its statutory powers including considering planning applications, the construction of highways, and the compulsory acquisition of land. The City Council has also embarked on a major programme of housing refurbishment within the Heartlands area.

The Board of BHL includes 7 members from the private sector and 4 representatives of the local authority. The strength of the BHL board and the commitment of its member partners is indicated by the fact that four of the five developers are represented by main board members of their respective firms. The City Council in turn is represented by equally authoritative figures including the Council Leader, the Chairman of its Economic Development Committee, and a senior opposition counsellor. The Chief Executive of Heartlands is on long-term secondment from the main board of Tarmac, the Finance Director and Company Secretary is provided by the City of Birmingham.

Birmingham Heartlands Limited has set up a sophisticated management structure to promote development, to realise the objectives of its private and public sector members, and to accommodate central government restrictions on local authority participation in private sector activities. BHL provides a strategic planning framework for the whole area, and this embraces social and economic initiatives as well as environmental improvement and property development. It operates on an annual budget of about £0.6 million provided proportionally by its member firms and the City Council. It commissions studies as required and also coordinates the activities of a number of topic working parties including: housing, roads/ infrastructure, environment and building refurbishment, training, land pooling and community trust development. There is also a committee to promote the Heartlands Education Compact, which covers private companies and eight local schools, and aims to provide job opportunities for school-leavers.

Each Heartlands working party is chaired by an appropriate board member, with secondees from member companies and the local authority, and feeds information and advice into the overall strategy and to the on-site development activities. In addition there are area working parties to oversee five major development projects within Heartlands. These are: a high tech and service area called Waterlinks, housing at Bordesley Village, an industrial area called Heartlands Industrial, offices, hotels, shops and a major art gallery at Star Site, and a large mixed development project at Fort Dunlop.

Originally it was thought that BHL itself would engage in development activities, but it became clear that this method of operation would fall foul of government restrictions on local authority participation. Now, in a more suitable arrangement, BHL provides the strategic planning framework, land pooling and other assistance to separate development consortia which in turn carry out development for each of the five main projects. Membership in these consortia is not confined to the partner-developers, although they have first option on participation. Other developers participate in the consortia and in other developments which they themselves may propose. Other joint venture partners are also consortia members, for example housing associations and building societies in Bordesley Village.

The Heartlands Initiative is now two years into a long-term strategic plan which looks ahead to the year 2000. Approximately £900 million worth of expenditure is earmarked for the five main developments. In addition another £280 million is budgeted for expenditure on Local Authority housing, roads and other infrastructure and land reclamation and business relocation expenses. A final financial arrangement within Heartlands also needs to be mentioned. This is the commitment of each development consortium to recycle ten per cent of profits back into BHL for its continuing operation, when profits begin to flow.

In conclusion, Heartlands is a unique, sophisticated vehicle for linking public and private sector interests in area-based regeneration. It is by no means a wholly property-led initiative: community regeneration schemes are established in the overall strategy. For the private sector it provides an opportunity to help shape the strategic vision and plans within which development projects will occur, and to help foster the marketability of those projects by area-wide improvements. The initial cost to the partner firms is a relatively minor annual cash contribution to BHL and a more substantial commitment of the seconded time of board members and other executives.

For the City of Birmingham Council, it achieves a working partnership, both management and financial, with the private sector towards shared urban regeneration goals, and an appropriate major role in the strategic planning for the area. It taps into major development expertise in the private sector, and is in a position to ensure local community participation in major development initiatives, and to supplement its own investment programme in housing and environmental improvement.

The partnership works because private and public sector partners have made very substantial commitments of top level management expertise, and because the large-area approach is likely to foster a critical mass of development activity and investor confidence in the longer term. There are lessons in good practice here for other cities where relations between city councils and conventional urban development corportions have been strained or antagonistic: development initiatives are likely to take off most effectively where there is genuine partnership between the private and public sector and local authorities are included in the relationship.

The Highbury Initiative and Birmingham City 2000
A three-way partnership between the City Council, central government's City Action Team (CAT), and the private sector is examining the role of the city centre in Birmingham's regeneration process. In 1988 the city council and the CAT organised an international symposium at a venue called Highbury on the link between the redevelopment of the city centre and the long-term economic prosperity of the wider city (Simms, 1989). Participants were asked to look beyond the immediate benefit of construction jobs for inner city residents to wider issues of robust, long-term prosperity and the quality of life for the hundreds of thousands of residents who visited the city centre for working or shopping.

In 1989 a second symposium was held, again organised by the City and the CAT, to take forward the initiative. Thirty-three Birmingham businesses attended. It was decided that instead of a general forum for promoting the city centre, a series of 'quarters' would be identified, for example the Jewellery Quarter and the Financial Quarter and relevant fora would be encouraged to develop on the basis of these designated areas.

Out of the Highbury Initiative there emerged Birmingham City 2000, a private sector-led initiative to boost Birminghams's image as financial centre, to broaden the skills base and ethnic background of support staff, to promote graduate recruitment, to lobby for environmental improvements and to assist in attracting venture capital to Birmingham. Within a few months of its inception 135 firms had paid the £100 entrance fee to Birmingham City 2000, which is managed by a small steering group of representatives of 12 firms, and chaired by a partner of KPMG Peat Marwick. City 2000 has also attracted further public funding from the CAT for a range of projects. One of the early projects of Birmingham City 2000 was to commission a research study to examine local, national and international perceptions of Birmingham.

Aston Science Park
One of the pioneering multi-sector partnerships has been the establishment of the Aston Science Park, opened in 1983. The Park is located on a 22 acre landscaped site in East Birmingham, adjacent to the Heartlands. The objective of the Science Park is to promote the development of high technology/knowledge based companies and to redevelop a hitherto derelict area of East Birmingham. In both areas the Science Park is successful, and around 1,000 employees now work in 65 companies in 220,000 sq ft of new office space. The proportion of employees from ethnic minorities exceeds that of Birmingham generally, although there are no quotas.

The corporate structure of Aston Science Park is based on Birmingham Technology Limited (BTL), a managing company for the Science Park. BTL is jointly owned by the City of Birmingham, Aston University and Lloyds Bank. The company has set up a venture capital subsidiary, BT (venture capital) Limited with an initial fund of £2 million, from equal contributions of the City and Lloyds. The Science Park provides both property and business development advice to companies. The property consists of fully fitted incubator units for new companies, and larger 'venture units' for expanding companies.

Advice comes from a multidisciplinary management team at BTL and from technical experts on the University faculty.

The pioneering success of Aston Science Park has meant that it has been adopted as a model for similar developments in Europe and North America. In particular the Director of BTL attributes its contribution to urban regeneration as a result of:

> the private sector ethos of BTL combined with the long-term perspective provided by the City of Birmingham Council.

Birmingham Training and Enterprise Council (TEC)
One further fledgling partnership needs to be mentioned. This is the Birmingham TEC, which in its own words:

> ...is a partnership of all organisations in Birmingham concerned with training, education and enterprise to drive a market led system which will furnish employers, providers and employees with training and support...

The TEC, which began operations in late 1990, has established 12 major Sector Compacts between employers and providers of training. These will build on the Local Employer Networks already established by the Chamber of Commerce, and their purpose is to develop relevant training targets for particular industry groups (such as engineering, construction, clerical etc) and relating skill developments to needs and the provision of common quality standards and programme criteria for Youth Training and Employment Training. The sector compacts will be linked to the initiatives of the Ten Company Group described above through a project worker funded by the CAT and TEC. In addition to the sector compacts the TEC has set up five generic sub-groups: equal opportunities, education, ethnic issues, women's issues and issues relevant to disabled people. The TEC also intends to set up in future an 'enterprise forum' to assist in small business development.

The Board of the TEC consists of eleven representatives from the private sector and other representatives from trade unions, education and the City of Birmingham. As well as the sector work, the TEC intends to operate as a strong lobby group for the needs of training. Three years of support from the Employment Department is guaranteed, and a secondment from the Rover Group has been announced.

Training in the inner city
Finally, mention should be made of a partnership venture in training for inner city residents, which provides an example of a project developed using the resources of public, voluntary and private sector organisations. The Handsworth Skills Partnership is an initiative involving a variety of organisations in funding and running a targeted management training programme for members of the black community in Handsworth. Set up in 1989, the Partnership delivers an accredited course leading to a Certificate in Management Studies. The Partnership's course is staffed by tutors at Matthew Boulton College; the project is managed by Action Resource Centre's Birmingham office; and the initiative has been funded by a combination of charitable foundations, two companies (British Telecom and IBM), and the Government's East Birmingham Task Force.

7.4 Overcoming constraints on good practice
During the course of this research a number of constraints on good practice of private sector involvement in urban regeneration were identified by respondents. These are reviewed briefly below.

Communication and coordination
Many firms expressed the view that their individual efforts should be all 'pulling in the same direction' towards some overall regeneration goals for Birmingham. There was concern that without better communication and coordination there would be duplication of effort and inefficiency among what was described as a 'mishmash and web of organisations'. As one respondent said:

> A critical issue for (our firm) is what are the needs of Birmingham's inner city and best to meet them. It's hard to assess this because there is no forum for considering overall needs and how different firms can contribute most cost-effectively.

The great majority of interviewees from private firms contacted expressed concern about their lack of knowledge of other urban regeneration initiatives in Birmingham.

There are many networks and initiatives in Birmingham involving the private sector in community investment, but no focus for coordination, debate at strategic level and information exchange. The gap could be filled by the development of a city-wide partnership forum, involving bodies such as the City Council, the new TEC, the CAT and the Chamber of Commerce. This should be relatively simple given the good networking already established between these bodies and others, especially through partnership ventures such as Heartlands. The forum could then form the kind of strategic 'overseer' body which many of our respondents would like to see. Moreover, on the Manchester model established in the Moss Side district, the forum could 'spin off' a business support group with a remit to coordinate business action and involvement in partnerships in Birmingham's inner city districts.

Such a development at the strategic level could be further complemented at the operational level by a local Per Cent Club to promote business contributions to the community; and by a 'funding forum' of the kind being developed in Bristol and Sheffield, bringing together voluntary sector umbrella groups, community trusts, local authority funding departments and business representatives to exchange information and coordinate action on particular projects. A Common Purpose programme was set up in Birmingham in 1990, and this should strengthen networking between key agencies in the city.

Secondments

One of the most important types of private sector contribution to urban regeneration in Birmingham is the seconding of experienced mid-career staff to urban initiatives, and a number described here are only made viable by secondments. However, there is serious concern that the supply of secondees is vulnerable to economic downturn, which is the very situation in which many projects particularly need the assistance and knowledge provided by secondees. There was also concern expressed by the Chamber of Commerce that the usual one-year secondments provided by firms were often too short, as the learning curve for secondees was very steep in the first year.

Secondees themselves confirmed that they and their firms often considerably underestimated the challenge of a posting to an urban regeneration programme, and that it was only after the first year that they felt they were 'starting to know the ropes' and beginning to make a substantial contribution. But a number of secondees said that at the very point when they started to make a substantial contribution, their position as a secondee also became tenuous because their companies viewed secondments as assignments of one year duration.

Government funding

Central government funding is clearly essential to many of the urban renewal initiatives described here. Many of the respondents expressed appreciation for that funding, for example through the CAT and Task Force, and its role in allowing initiatives to get off the ground. But equally there was widespread concern that, in an effort to transfer more responsibility to the private sector, the tapering of funding to what is usually a complete cut-off after three years was too restrictive a policy:

> Initiatives barely get off the ground before expensive staff time must be devoted, not to urban renewal, but to raising funds in a desperate attempt to stay in business.

That urban regeneration may benefit from a long-term commitment to funding is suggested by the case of Glasgow, where the Scottish Office, through the Scottish Development Agency and the Housing Corporation in Scotland (now Scottish Homes), has steadily funded urban initiatives for more than a decade.

Respondents also referred to limitations on training provision stemming from restrictions on public funds. Representatives from smaller firms felt that the resources available for training purposes were insufficient, and that in the event of the current economic downturn becoming worse they were likely to go out of government sponsored training altogether. One said training 'could go by the board because of the meagre resources'. Another manager from a firm training many residents from ethnic minorities commented:

> Our commercial training rate is £450 per day for equipment and operator. For government sponsored training we get £130 per day. It doesn't pay but we're giving something back to the community. But I don't know for how much longer. It's sad really, we could do so much more.

Infrastructure policy

A number of respondents from major firms involved in urban renewal initiatives expressed almost vehement concern that central government did not appreciate fully the potential benefits to be derived from coordination of major infrastructure investments, mainly in road and rail transport, towards urban regeneration objectives, particularly if these could be assessed in a national and regional development framework. A few respondents mentioned that they where worried that without such a strategic perspective the potential benefits for

Birmingham from developments such as the Channel Tunnel would be lost.

The key point raised by these and similar comments is the need to see inner city problems and renewal initiatives in a holistic way and not cut them off from broader strategic considerations of city-wide issues. Urban renewal needs to be about initiatives for the whole city and programmes targeted on inner city districts are best developed within a wider strategic framework.

The role of local government
A number of respondents expressed concern at the growing constraints on the freedom of action of the City of Birmingham Council. They noted that many of the partnership initiatives which were proving so instrumental in Birmingham's recovery would now be impossible, such as the Aston Science Park initiative and the development of the NEC. In particular, constraints on local government capital expenditure, and the ability to spend capital receipts, were seen as obstacles to renewal efforts in the inner city. One respondent from a major UK developer suggested a special inner city development zone, similar to a simplified planning zone, in which local government and business would be freed from the financial constraints on partnerships imposed by central government and particularly the Treasury.

Conclusion
The sheer number of initiatives in Birmingham with some form of business involvement suggest that the private sector is making a substantial contribution to urban regeneration. A number of these initiatives, such as IMI's Holford Estate, the Ten Company Group and the Aston Science Park are already providing a model for initiatives in other cities in Britain. Other initiatives, such as Birmingham Heartlands, could also provide a model of the kind of sophisticated organisational arrangements necessary to make a substantial and lasting contribution to the needs of urban regeneration in inner cities, and to the means for successfully marrying private initiative to public reponsibility.

It is also obvious that much of Birmingham's success in urban regeneration is neither private-led nor public-led, but is the result of partnerships between the public sector, with the City Council especially prominent, and the private sector, often led by the Chamber of Commerce. It is unlikely that many of the initiatives described here would have come into being or succeeded without this partnership approach and without the commitment of leading organisations in the public and private sectors.

Most of the constraints on urban regeneration described by interviewees, and listed above, fall within the responsibility of central government and require no further comment. However, two areas for action involving the private sector stand out. First, companies should recognise that secondments are a substantial contribution to urban regeneration but may require a two to three year commitment to realise maximum benefit, and that they can gain from this as well as the agencies and groups to which their staff are assigned. Second, the City Council, the TEC, the Chamber of Commerce and other key agencies such as the CAT could join in setting up the high level forum for strategic coordination which many companies would like to see. From this other regular fora could be established to help coordinate local operations, especially for the inner areas outside the city centre, and to assist communication. Many firms and other agencies would appreciate developments of this kind.

7.5 Selected case studies

The following section offers two detailed case studies of firms in Birmingham, IMI and the Rover Group, both of which have extensive involvement in urban regeneration efforts. A number of other good practice case studies for the West Midlands are available in a report prepared for DTI by Ernst and Young (1990).

IMI plc

IMI is a major international group of 80 firms with a turnover in excess on £1 billion, headquartered at a 220 acre site at Witton in Birmingham. IMI develops and manufactures a wide range of advanced materials and high technology products. In addition to a extensive plant in Birmingham's inner area, it has subsidary companies worldwide and major plants elsewhere in the UK, North and South America, Continental Europe and Australia. IMI's companies operate in five main areas: building products, fluid power, special engineering, drinks dispensing, and refined and wrought metals, such as titanium alloys. Operations in Birmingham include IMI Group Headquarters, IMI Components, IMI Titanium, Eley, Eley

Hawk, Holford Estates, Witton Estates Management Services and IMI Computing, all at the company's Witton location near the Aston Villa football ground and adjacent to the Birmingham Heartlands area. IMI has also acquired the Birmingham Mint near the Witton site.

IMI's corporate policies relevant to urban regeneration in Birmingham fall into two areas of activity: education, training and social policy; and derelict land and economic regeneration.

Education, training and social policy
IMI's corporate policy is intended to give a high priority to education and training to ensure competitiveness. They run a training unit, IMI Training Services, and an Engineering Training Centre, both in Birmingham. IMI also gives high priority to the economic regeneration of local areas and communities around their plants to ensure a supply of skilled employees. Both aspects of policy are viewed in terms of enlightened self-interest, and good longer term business sense. An IMI Managing Director makes the point:

> The training and development of employees at all levels are major factors affecting a company's ability to adapt and respond effectively to changes in its business environment. Training is an important investment activity in which Britain lags behind its international competitors.

IMI Training Services offers 67 courses in management, manufacturing, communications, marketing, computing, finance, office skills and project control to IMI employees and to other customers of their services. Residents from local ethnic minority communities, reached via IMI activities in local schools, in careers work, at mosques and churches, and at job clubs and community centres, are particularly encouraged to take part in clerical, administrative and engineering training schemes offered by IMI.

The IMI Engineering Training Centre trains apprentices, craftsmen, technicians and graduate engineers. The Centre is designated an approved training organisation by the Employment Department. IMI makes particular effort to recuit Afro-Caribbean and Asian trainees. This commitment is also reflected in their training manager's participation in the Extended Group of Ten Companies, described above. Similar commitment is also reflected in the fact that an IMI main board director is a member of the board of the new

Birmingham TEC, and that a managing director of an operating unit sits on the Wolverhampton TEC board.

Finally, IMI in Birmingham also has a particular commitment to the disabled, and has provided free premises for special training programmes for disabled people.

Derelict land and economic regeneration
In discussing what amounts to IMI's one company urban regeneration programme, their training manager noted that:

> The most understated asset in Birmingham is a skilled manufacturing workforce close by in the inner city.

To take advantage of this under-utilised asset, and to make use of a large parcel of land in Witton surplus to their needs due to manufacturing rationalisation, IMI decided to embark on a long-term plan to develop a high quality landscaped business park from a heavily polluted 110 acre site. The three fold objective of the company set up to do the work, Holford Estates Ltd., was to reclaim derelict land, adjacent to the Heartlands area described above, for the most appropriate economic use; to provide a source of employment in the local community; and in the medium to long term to generate income from the new asset.

IMI was able to take the long-term view necessary, particularly to ride through periods of depressed property prices, but as for most derelict industrial land, a measure of subsidy was necessary for land reclaimation and economic viability. IMI therefore negotiated £5.8 million of DoE Urban Development Grant funding towards a £28 million investment programme for what was to be known as Holford Estates. The intention was to develop an extensivly landscaped, high quality estate at rents higher than normal speculative developments in the area, thus securing tenants likely to remain for long periods. In this IMI has been successful: 665,000 square feet of developments have been constructed or reserved for tenants and over 1,450 jobs created by firms, some not previously located in the West Midlands or even in Britain.

A second phase covering 37 acres has been planned and negotiations are in hand with the DoE to secure the necessary grant aid to make the development viable. Another 1,500 jobs are expected to result. At the same time some of the remaining low grade industrial buildings at Holford are being let to small or start-up businesses such as joiners and pipefitters on renewable short-term arrangements.

In an effort to link new job availability with local community needs, IMI also links its training programme to the requirements of incoming employers to Holford. Also part of the Holford development is a three acre plot of land situated by the River Tame which has been set aside as an ecology area to create an urban woodland. The success of the Holford landscaping programme is such that local people use the area as parkland.

Finally, there is one other facet of IMI's urban regeneration commitment which should be touched upon. This is the transfer of urban regeneration skills into and out of what is first and foremost a manufacturing company. IMI's Corporate Services Manager was on the board of the Black Country Development Corporation, and some current staff at the nearby Birmingham Heartlands venture have previously benefited from working for IMI at the Holford development.

IMI is clearly a firm which takes a very broad perspective on what constitutes enlightened self interest. In particular their efforts at Holford combined with their commitment to community training provides an unusual example of an urban regeneration effort undertaken by a single firm. What stands out in particular is IMI's understanding of enlightened self interest in a long-term, strategic perspective, of substantial benefit to the wider community, the economy of the city and themselves. IMI's experience also underlines the point that grant subsidy for derelict land reclamation is essential to private sector development, and that central government has an important support role here.

The Rover Group

In the discussion above of the pioneering work of the Ten Company Group, and the extension of this concept, mention was made of the important role of The Rover Group in this inter-firm partnership effort, not least its commitment to fund a portion of the initiative. This is one example of Rover's corporate policy, which is committed to increasing the training and employment opportunities of Birmingham's ethnic minority residents.

The Rover Group initiated an equal opportunities review in 1987 by growing internal recognition of the importance of youth training and after a review revealed that only about 9 per cent of Rover's trainees at their Longbridge and Drews Lane plants in Birmingham were from ethnic minorities. The company looked closely at its trainee applications and rejections. This showed that 8 per cent of the applications were from ethnic minorities, and a slightly higher number, 9 per cent, were taken on as trainees. The problem was not that ethnic minority applicants were disadvantaged once in the system, but that they were not applying in sufficient numbers. Rover decided to take action through the Ten Company Group with the result that the proportion of ethnic minority trainees has increased to over 20 per cent in three years.

In particular Rover questioned its recruitment and selection practices and found that tradition and word of mouth recruiting restricted recruitment to the mainly white neighbourhoods in the vicinity of the very large Longbridge plant, with 18,000 employees, which takes the vast majority of Rover's trainees in Birmingham. Rover therefore revised its recruitment policy towards one of positive action, based on the perception that it was part of a larger urban community which included other, more distant neighbourhoods with high proportions of ethnic minority residents.

Virtually every secondary school in Birmingham was targeted for recruitment. Equally important, Rover drew on the advice of ethnic minority representatives on the Ten Company Group to revise its whole application, interviewing and selection procedures to make them more 'user friendly' to potential applicants from ethnic minorities. As Rover's Training Administration Manager puts it:

> This was not just a marketing exercise, it was also an exercise in building up relationships with the ethnic minority communities.

This was done by giving talks at schools, and sponsoring Careers Conventions, including at the Birmingham Central Mosque and other locations relevant to Asian and Afro-Caribbean residents. A key to the whole initiative was the establishment of a programme of systematic ethnic monitoring to enable Rover to assess its performance. Finally much of these initiatives were carried out within the framework of the Ten Company Group and Rover's policy has been to contribute, along with its partner firms, substantially to the Group's initiatives. The contribution has included overhead costs, secondment time, and support for the printing of the books that resulted, for example, 5,000 copies of *Saying Yes*.

Such community linkages are just one part of Rover's community policy, which also includes:

- Education Partnerships including students on work experience, teachers on secondment to Rover, the provision of industrial tutors to schools, encouragement to Rover employees to become school governors, work with Careers Services, and direct investment of matching funds annually into a number of 'Rover Rooms' in schools, which may be for library facilities, computing facilities, computer design and technology or for other purposes (two schools in 1990).
- Charitable donations both by the company directly to community groups, for example for playground facilities for handicapped children, and also by a 3 pence deduction weekly from the pay packet of every employee, administered by a Charity Committee, mainly composed of shop stewards.
- Voluntary activities and secondment of staff, for example encouragement of employees to become involved in activities such as Meals on Wheels or other activities which they may suggest.

Finally, during the early 1990s, Rover is extending its policy of community linkages, from a focus mainly on young people, to adults requiring pre-entry training, and to the opportunities of improving the career progression of ethnic minority employees into management.

Messages on good practice

Rover's range of activities covers not only traditional 'charitable giving' but also extends into areas of mainstream commercial activity such as training, where the company's policy links its own recruitment needs and procedures with the interests of local ethnic minority communities. This is a good example of a company building up a varied but coherent portfolio of community investment activities which integrate 'community affairs' with mainstream business strategy. The overall policy also exemplifies good practice in that it involves employees at all levels, and reaches out to other firms and agencies to form partnerships which add value to the company's own activities. The involvement with the Ten Company Group is a striking example of innovative inter-firm partnership which provides a framework for changes in in-house procedures and new community initiatives by the individual company.

8 Case Study: Bristol

8.1 Introduction

The outstanding impression gained from the case studies in Bristol is of resilience and promise for the future, and this is a reflection of many new initiatives and developments. Informants recall 'complacency' and 'conservatism' in Bristol until well into the 1980s, and there is a record of failed or half-hearted action when the city's recent problems first became apparent. Historically, however, Bristol has a tradition of adapting successfully as one part of its economic base declines and another takes its place, and this is now happening again.

The local labour market area in Bristol is the County of Avon rather than the city alone, and travel to work is both ways. In 1981, 21 per cent of all Bristol City men in employment and 37 per cent of those in manufacturing worked outside the city. The county's economic basis changed considerably during the 1980s. From 1981 to 1989 manufacturing employment fell by 21 per cent, with particularly sharp declines in tobacco, food and drink, paper and printing, and aerospace, and manufacturing's share in total employment fell from 27 per cent to under 20 per cent. This, however, was more than offset by an increase in service employment, most notably of 75 per cent in insurance, banking, finance, and business services. Although unemployment in the Bristol travel to work area reached 10-11 per cent between 1982 and 1986, it fell back by June 1990 to 4.3 per cent. In 1989 (Table 1) Bristol was in the top 15 per cent of the 280 local labour markets in Britain on an index of employment and economic prosperity: lower, but still above the median, on an index of improvement in the previous four years: on either index, the city is far ahead of Birmingham or Manchester.

However, although Bristol is not a 'problem city' in the same sense as London and some northern cities, it is still certainly a city with problems, economic and social.

Table 1 **Employment and strength of the economy in four local labour market areas: rank order out of 280 LLMAs in Great Britain**

	1989	Index of improvement in position 1985-89
Bristol	66	130
Manchester	156	206
Birmingham	203	219
Sheffield	210	239

Source: Tony Champion and Anne Green, *Local Economic Performance in Britain During the Late Eighties*, Booming Towns, 1990.

Unemployment in the spring of 1990 was still over 8 per cent in a belt of city wards running down from the Bristol Task Force area, north of the Avon, to the city's southern boundary. In parts of the Task Force area it is over three times the average for the city. There is a certain shabbiness about central Bristol: the generally run-down state of certain wards, large areas of derelict or semi-derelict industrial or railway land, the old-fashioned and unattractive style of Bristol's main shopping centre at Broadmead, along with under-development of arts and leisure facilities: hardly, as one informant put it, a bright-light city centre to attract incoming managers. North-South communications are poor, which among other things has an impact on unemployment: many of the new jobs are in the north while many of the unemployed are in the south, and there was said to be a Bristol rule that workers other than professionals or managers are reluctant to travel more than half an hour to work.

There are problems of training and motivation: low qualifications, discrimination and poor motivation were identified as difficulties in the areas of relatively high unemployment, while on the other hand the Avon Training and Enterprise Council (TEC) sees as its central problem the need for a much higher level of training for the 95 per cent of the work force who are in work – as its Newsletter for July 1990 suggests, anything up to a ten-fold increase in local employers' expenditure on training if they are to keep pace with competitors overseas. The enterprise agency, New Work Trust, similarly sees its chief task as no longer to assist people into self-employment but to help already established small businesses to compete and grow.

There are also, of course, the problems of housing shortage, community development, and social welfare to be expected in any large city. Issues of race relations were highlighted by the St. Paul's riots – 'half a mile up the road', as one company noted in giving the reasons for its community contributions policy – but informants insisted that the ethnic element in Bristol's problems, though important, should not be over-stressed.

How effectively have the private and public sectors acted, separately or together, to identify and solve problems like these? The period of what many respondents referred to as the city's 'complacency' is still recent. The contrast in Table 1 between Bristol's ranking on prosperity in a given year and on improvement over the previous years is a useful reminder. There is a history of failed initiatives for the regeneration of Bristol: some which are now taking off made a hesitant start, as with plans for an Avon light rail network; others were taken up and dropped, as with proposals for a spine road to by-pass the North-South bottleneck. That history has left a legacy of scepticism towards new initiatives. But the major finding of this case study is that the climate and effectiveness of action now seem to have changed for the better.

8.2 Companies and their community links
American as well as British experience shows not only that companies do not follow any standard pattern of community investment but that, given the differences between their stages of development, their market circumstances and the communities in which they operate, there are good reasons why they should not do so. The key question to ask about any company is whether its policies are reasoned and effective in the light of its own circumstances. This question was explored with eleven companies (chosen on local advice from the Bristol Task Force and other informants as to companies known to be making a significant community contribution).

The sample of firms contacted includes large and medium-companies and one which is very small, but differences in size matter for the purposes of this report less than might be thought, since we have looked primarily at companies' *local* contribution. Companies such as British Telecom or IBM are national leaders in community investment, with budgets running into millions of pounds, highly developed policies and procedures, and, by the standards usual in this field, large and specialised staffs. Comparisons with companies of that kind can be intimidating to others that are smaller and less far along the road. When it comes to decisions by local management about community investment, however, the scale of operation of companies like these may be nothing out of the ordinary. British Telecom is the biggest corporate donor in the country, but Telecom Severnside in 1989/90 had a regional budget well within the reach of even a medium-sized firm, managed part-time by one manager with an assistant. The grants which it made out of it, to over a hundred charities and forty community projects, were often of a size within the reach of even a small company. Even a traditionally expensive service like seconding a manager – a long-term secondment 'might be equivalent to an investment of £100,000' (IBM) – can be, and in Bristol is being, re-designed by Action Resource Centre to be within the reach of modest professional partnerships.

Local managers in a large company may of course be able to persuade national management to back a big local project, and also to draw on headquarter resources for guidance on the reasons and procedures for contributing. But smaller companies too can work out reasoned policies on their own and make, by local standards, a significant contribution. A good illustration of how to do both is provided by the smallest company in our sample, Mosaic Management Consulting Group, which is the subject of a detailed case study in section 8.5 below.

Motivation and general level of commitment
What companies devote to community investment is liable to come out of several budgets and to be governed by a mixture of motivations. One manager said, 'No one is purely philanthropic', but in contributing to the community no one is purely commercial either. We always found a combination of a sense of social responsibility and of 'something in it for us', but with differing emphases between

companies and the various areas of involvement. Lloyds Bank's sponsorship guidelines define sponsorship as 'a combination of promotional activity and community support', but with a strong accent on promotion – marrying hard-nosed business with benefit to the community, as a Lloyds manager said – whereas its donations guidelines speak first of putting some of the company's profits back into the community and improving the quality of life, and only then of 'implicit recognition of the advantages of a well-balanced society in which to pursue our business objectives'. Harveys of Bristol has on one side a programme of sponsorship in the arts, especially music, to benefit the community and promote the image of quality in the company's products through association with quality performance in the arts ('one classic deserves another'); and on the other a wider-ranging programme for 'putting something back into the community' through charitable donations. Sun Life noted the balance in their work experience programmes between response to demand from the schools and the company's own interest in recruitment.

In the 'hard-nosed business' areas such as sponsorship there is a business interest by which to decide what is to be done and monitor performance. In charitable giving and general community support the criteria are harder to pin down: in Lloyds this was reflected in more centralised control of this type of spending than of sponsorship. The two extremes, in our sample, were IBM and Interlink Express. In IBM, according to our respondent, 'We often used to chuck charity over the wall': now 'charity' is downplayed, the firm's community activity is seen as a form of investment, community affairs clients are dealt with as they would be if they were 'mainstream' business customers, and visibility for the company is an important objective.

In Interlink, by contrast, the accent is very much on social responsibility and 'putting something back into the community', with only a marginal public relations element. Sun Life described its philosophy as enlightened self-interest, but also noted how its balance of emphasis had shifted in the last few years from self-interest, as with an insurance company's obvious concern with medical research, towards a more 'enlightened' long range approach, though without leaving shorter term self-interest out of account. In this perspective, the company should contribute to solving Bristol's problems, in its capacity as a major local employer with a stake in stability and prosperity: 'the riots were half a mile up the road... We cannot operate a successful business in a disturbed community'.

More accidental factors also play a part in policy development. It may matter a good deal where budget decisions are made. For instance, Hewlett Packard has a local reputation for its policy on school-business links and donations of product, but less so for cash donations: these are determined, not company-wide, but by what individual managers can spare out of the tightly controlled budgets for their own cost centres. Personalities also count for a great deal in the development of some companies' approaches to community involvement. Sun Life doubled its profits between 1985 and 1989 but multiplied its community contributions five times (six times by 1990), and the point of departure was a memorandum by one director who felt that the company's standard of giving was 'poor'. In RS Alliance community investment has 'become part of the company ethos', but this goes back, again, to a director whose own experience in public relations and marketing convinced him that local community involvement should be an essential part of business, and notably of his field of business: one which among other things raises the standing of his type of company with clients.

The practical conclusion from these considerations is that the establishment of a norm for the level of community contributions, as promoted by the Per Cent Club, is necessary. The criteria for spending on general community investment are mixed and imprecise, and the level at which it is set is within wide limits arbitrary, even where, as in IBM, this type of involvement has a strong business component. Companies need 'something to latch on to': a standard which is realistic in the light of what, for example, the upper quartile of companies involved in community investment actually achieve – and this is approximately the Per Cent Club standard.

What and where companies contribute

What and where companies contribute depends on their own interests and potential. Hewlett Packard and IBM (through its dealer network) give computers; Harveys of Bristol give bottles of wine; Sun Life, with a lot of furniture and equipment to dispose of, is an active supporter of Business Links; Gateway is specially interested in involvement of staff and customers in and around its 730 stores, and Telecom Severnside and Lloyds also distribute their local donations widely 'to be perceived as part of the local scenery'; and all of these companies also back larger local projects out of national funds. Interlink, which is not a high street firm, makes mainly national donations. It deliberately does not favour its headquarters area in Bristol, whereas Gateway, which is also a Bristol company, has made some very large local donations. Telecom, Sun Life, and IBM have targeted some or most of their local involvement on the inner city: other companies were not specially concerned with the inner city and the Task Force area and had to be tempted in. Wimpey has established a training centre in St. Paul's in association with the Construction Industry Training Board for ET-based courses. Other local employers are being involved in customised pre-recruitment training and interview guarantee schemes.

A number of key points on good practice emerged from the company interviews:

Leading from strength
The easiest form of company involvement, it has been said, is to write a cheque. That may in fact be the best thing to do in particular cases, but best practice covers a great deal more: gifts of product and equipment, supply of facilities (Sun Life originally housed ARC Avon, and pays for its new office since it had to change premises), supply of expertise through secondments or the professional advice which New Work Trust obtains from its associated companies, or RS Alliance's contribution, as a public relations and marketing firm, to the 'catalysing' activities of the new Business Leadership Team, The Bristol Initiative. Hewlett Packard made the point about leading from strength particularly clearly. Their first priority is for committing their skills in information technology: next, giving their equipment, which is cost-effective to receivers as well as good public relations for the company: cash donations come third.

Involving employees and franchisees
Mosaic involves employees directly and advantageously in the company's own contributions programme, and so to a degree may other companies. But we heard more about companies' support for employee giving as such, and on this we received a very clear message. Payroll giving (GAYE) by itself is neither popular nor successful, but collective fund-raising events by employees themselves are productive, 'fun' and, as in Mosaic, good for the company. Several of

our companies match employee fund-raising pound for pound. Employee volunteering was often encouraged, though usually in employees' own time, but IBM and Mosaic allow use of work time for community activities: there are no precise rules for this, but in practice, as was said by IBM, employees find that community involvement counts in their career development just as it does in Mosaic. Interlink and IBM in different ways involve their dealers (IBM) or franchisees (Interlink) as well as employees in community action.

Hewlett Packard made a general suggestion which deserves to be followed up. Its parent in the United States is a leader in the United Way movement. Local United Ways integrate payroll giving, other forms of fund-raising, and companies' own contributions into a package of collective action which generates enthusiasm, strong support from companies (notably through secondments for United Way campaigns) as well as from employees (volunteering as well as cash donations), and large amounts of cash for community causes: and the United Way system has the means to ensure that these are effectively assessed and monitored. Should Britain, it was suggested, not follow this road? The existing community trusts and charitable foundations could be a mechanism for development of integrated 'packages' for the private sector, given suitable resources for marketing to companies.

8.3 Partnerships and networks.

Companies' contribution to community investment is not simply a matter of what companies do on their own, nor even of participation in joint activities, like enterprise agencies, to which they have been recruited by one of the intermediary bodies. A further question is, how far do companies themselves take initiatives towards building networks for coordination of community action and information exchange, or feeding ideas into them? Our sample was biased by its method of selection, for the firms we contacted are by definition active companies: a few were indifferent, but most were contributing to the operation of networks and agencies in a variety of ways.

Companies and the local networks

Good practice implies a two-way relation between companies and local networks and agencies such as those described below. The networks need the support of companies, but the companies also need the networks.

Our Bristol sample was chosen from companies known to be active in the community, and most – though one or two were indifferent – were contributing to local networks and agencies at either the strategic or the operating level, and in a variety of ways. There was significant personal involvement by senior managers. IBM's external affairs manager for the South-West, for example, had 'made it his business to become part of the local networks'. Companies were providing business or professional advice, secondments, facilities or premises (as with Sun Life's assistance to ARC Avon), and of course money. Project funding tended to be preferred, but the Greater Bristol Trust owes a great deal to the four companies (including Harveys and Hewlett Packard) which contributed substantially in 1989/90 to its 'core' funding, and to those like Mosaic which are helping to build its endowment.

As with other forms of community involvement, the motive for helping to build and maintain the networks turned out to be a mixture of public spirit and self-interest, and examples quoted below make this clear. The personal involvement of a number of business leaders which we observed went well beyond what could be explained in terms of any direct contribution to their companies' bottom line. We were told at national level in IBM that, in choosing projects to support, dissemination – spreading the gospel of good practice – is a key consideration, as it is also in the Per Cent Club; and networking is one important means of doing this.

Networking may also, however, have a direct commercial purpose, as in the case of the retailers who collaborate in redeveloping the Broadmead shopping centre or the companies on the Brislington industrial estate who combined to improve recruitment through links with local schools. It may provide useful commercial contacts, and at least one local enterprise agency capitalises strongly on this for attracting sponsors interested in doing business with the small firms which the agency is helping to grow. For shaping their own community policies companies need outside information and strategic guidance such as networking can provide. The companies which we interviewed were far from being uninformed givers – that is why they were selected – but several company informants were still worried about the multiplicity and confusion of initiatives in Bristol. The networks and agencies operating in Bristol are, as will be shown, building up an increasingly coherent strategy for the city, but informants saw a need for more effort to project a coherent picture back to companies: notably, though not only, in the area of information about the needs of and services provided by community groups and other voluntary bodies.

We discuss below the range of partnerships in Bristol involving groups of companies, and the organisations in which business plays a role in partnership with bodies from other sectors.

Multi-firm partnerships
The Bristol Chamber of Commerce (3,000 current members) is of course long-established, but within the last year has taken what a number of respondents saw as a new, more open and dynamic course under a new chief executive and president. The CBI is also more active in Avon than in some other localities.

There are a number of more localised business networks. One is the Avon Valley Traders' Association, a group which is taking a leading part in regenerating the main shopping centre in the Development Corporation area. This grouping was encouraged by BDC as a partner for communication and constructive discussion.

Another multi-firm partnership is the Brislington Traders' Association based on an industrial estate. This body arose out of employers' concern about recruitment of young people in a somewhat isolated area, and has also been encouraged by the County Council as a contributor to its network of school-business links.

At the level of 'strategic' networking several of the companies visited were involved, and some very actively. This is partly a matter of local and personal attitudes. British Telecom, as a major employer, is involved in Bristol as it is elsewhere. IBM's external affairs manager for the South-West was among other things acting chief executive and fund-raiser for the Bristol Initiative Business Leadership Team at its inception. The managing director of RS Alliance was a prime mover as well in the establishment of the Bristol Initiative and is a member of its board: his motivation came from previous involvement with charity work and a feeling, shared by staff and clients, that Bristol needed more action for urban renewal, especially in view of the major racial problems in the inner city.

Multi-sector partnerships involving business

Over and above formal promotional or partnership agencies, we have learned to look for 'mafias', informal networks of influential people whose names appear in different capacities, and who bridge gaps between different organisations and may be the 'movers and shakers' in getting new initiatives off the ground. Common Purpose's community leadership programmes are aimed at the systematic development of such networks, but in Bristol, at the time of our survey, Common Purpose was only at the stage of a first approach. It has since established a programme for the city. Bristol does, however, have an informal 'mafia', radiating out from an inner circle of perhaps twenty or thirty people in the public and private sectors through a variety of networks both old (like that of the local solicitors) and new. Like so many other things in Bristol, this network is being renewed. The older network was seen by many informants as too complacent and limited in its range of thinking and action: but the same informants stressed that it is being rejuvenated as new companies move into the city and new and sharper business leaders come to the top.

A new business leadership team, the Bristol Initiative (TBI), was set up in 1989 based on the model for partnership ventures set out in the CBI's *Initiatives Beyond Charity* (1988). It is a business-based partnership, for it also involves the chief executives of the city and county and has representation from the Employment Service, the TUC, the University and Polytechnic, and the Church of England. The Bristol Initiative is described in detail in a separate case study in section 8.5 below.

A Bristol-Avon Economic Development Forum brings the Chamber of Commerce and the CBI together with the local authorities, the University and the Polytechnic. In an earlier and more limited form this association dates back to the 1970s, but became moribund: the Forum is effectively a new body established within the last two years.

There is a multiplicity of organisations in Bristol appealing for partnership activities and community investment from limited business funds. We identify below only some of the main agencies concerned with partnership with the private sector in the city's regeneration initiatives.

The local authorities, especially the Bristol City Council (Labour) and the Avon County Council (hung), both currently charge-capped. The city and county have obviously a very wide potential for contributing to development, and have in fact contributed in many ways, but informants tended to draw a distinction about where in these authorities the contribution comes from. Officers were seen as competent and involved, but leadership at member level was often felt to be weak, divided, and sometimes sectarian, irrespective of party. We do better in partnership activities, one business leader said, when councillors are not involved. The activities of both authorities are currently limited by charge-capping as well as capital expenditure controls.

There are two public agencies for local development, the government's Bristol Task Force (established in 1986) and the Bristol Development Corporation (1989). The Task Force's focus is on employment, training, enterprise, and urban regeneration in three inner city wards (Ashley, Easton, and Lawrence Hill) to the north of the Avon: part, but far from the whole, of the belt of unemployment defined in section 8.1 above. The Task Force has worked on partnership projects with business, the Employment Service, voluntary agencies and local authorities, focussing on training needs in its area. A notable partnership initiative in the area is the Westmorland Trust Technology Centre, in operation since November 1989: this is an open learning centre for office skills, funded by the Task Force, Avon County Council and IBM (which has provided substantial resources in the form of managerial advice, computer hardware and software). The Westmorland Trust itself is a Community Development Trust (similar to the Moss Side and Hulme CDT – see Chapter 9) with a remit to provide a forum for all local actors engaged in developing regeneration projects. It has a full time director and new board members from the private sector.

The Bristol Development Corporation's remit is to regenerate one and a half square miles of 'run-down buildings, industrial wasteland, and badly located businesses' mainly South of the Avon, with only a marginal overlap with the Task Force area. The BDC is the newest and smallest of the UDCs in England and Wales. It is managing a city centre spine road project (using private and public funds) and has recently begun dialogue with voluntary sector groups. The BDC was greeted with suspicion at first by many in the city, but has won a high reputation for rapid and effective action in partnership with small as well as larger businesses and its developing links with the voluntary sector appear to be promising.

More specialised agencies include the new Avon TEC and several enterprise agencies, of which the New Work Trust is outstanding, and other agencies like ARC Avon (secondments, training for community development, and 'business links' for gifts of furniture and equipment to voluntary organisations) and the Industrial Society (customised pre-recruitment training). The TEC has only just begun operations, and is a partnership venture involving companies, business umbrella groups, the local enterprise agencies, county and district councils and others.

In the voluntary sector, the Greater Bristol Trust (established in 1987) is a channel for 'federated giving' to charities by businesses or individuals: approaching two-thirds of its over 200 donors in 1989/90 were businesses. It has also been a focus for organised action by the voluntary sector. It assisted in assembling a Voluntary Sector Forum for dialogue with the Bristol Development Corporation, and has initiated a Grant Givers Forum for exchange of information and discussion of policies among major grant givers operating in the city. It is now building an endowment to give it a more solid base and a reliable flow of core and free income, and has succeeded in attracting one of the three major 'challenge grants' made available by the Charities Aid Foundation and the Charles Stewart Mott Foundation of the USA. The active and effective role of the Trust and its Director in the local networks was widely recognised by respondents.

To date the partnerships which have emerged have had little time to build up initiatives and experience. The focus of activity has been on infrastructural projects, employment issues and increasing local competitiveness. Within this mainly economic emphasis, the agencies have different strategic visions: of new dimensions to enterprise, training, and employment, of new commercial ventures and development for a 'brighter Bristol'. BDC has its vision of a Bristol Covent Garden complementary to the Broadmead centre; there are also initiatives for improvements in infrastructure, transport (BDC has secured approval and private as well as public finance for the North-South spine road), or in the supply of rented housing (TBI is beginning to consider this area), or in the regeneration of run-down areas. These visions do tend to complement each other, and cover between them the range of economic and infrastructural problems briefly outlined above. There has been no overall and authoritative assessment of Bristol's economy and its potential to pull the threads together, but the Bristol Avon Economic Forum has now commissioned the Polytechnic to provide one.

The TEC, similarly, has 'locked in' key parties, including the local authorities, enterprise agencies, and private sector companies, and works with and through a range of other agencies and networks. The Chamber of Commerce has, as noted above, changed under new management to a more open and cooperative relationship to other agencies. 'We sat down and talked in a civilised way', as one business leader said about the Chamber's relation to TBI, and the Chamber realised that TBI's work was complementary to its own and is now in full support of it. BDC is seen by some as a 'bulldozer', but does act as one of the catalysts, as illustrated by its promotion of the Avon Valley Traders' association and its systematic approach to and dialogue with the voluntary sector bodies such as Greater Bristol Trust.

Cooperation by and with the local authorities was said to be improving, though still dependent on personal contacts – made, for example, through the leadership of particular committees. An outstanding example of 'catalysing' is the county's brokering of business-school links. Another is the way in which the City is building a Civic Arts Trust as a vehicle for involving the private sector more in an under-developed field. Chief executives of the local authorities have been brought into TBI; the Bristol-Avon Forum has been revived; the Broadmead project brings together the local authorities and the traders; and the Avon light rail network seems to be on the way to development.

Operating partnerships: approaching the private sector
The test of the agencies is not merely whether they are coherent but whether they are operationally efficient, especially, for the purposes of this report, in involving the private sector. There have been some uncertain beginnings, but again the picture in late 1990 is generally promising. Looking at the range of agencies, four points stand out about the way in which good practice is developing in Bristol.

'*Investment, not charity*' – the quotation is from the Task Force, but the concept runs right through the work of the agencies: not only of the primarily economic agencies but, on the side of the voluntary organisations, that of GBT. 'We are always trying to get away from the idea of the hand-out to that of giving a service to the corporate sector': this is exactly the kind of relationship for which the

Development Corporation is looking in developing its policy towards the voluntary sector. ARC Avon said of its re-designed programme for secondments to voluntary organisation, 'we are no longer holding out the begging bowl' but promoting a type of secondment which gives clear benefits to companies, in terms of career development, as well as to receivers, and can be accurately monitored as a business proposition. The motive of social responsibility is recognised, but the accent is primarily on enlightened self-interest.

Self-sufficiency rather than subsidy is a key objective. ARC Avon, for example, may be able to move from a free and subsidised service in promoting secondments to charging companies for its services – but if so, it was underlined, charging to the training rather than the community relations budget. The New Work Trust is critical of other enterprise agencies which still rely on subsidy and the 'gift relationship'. It has not itself asked its 260 supporting companies for cash since 1981. It involves them as providers of professional expertise on the basis of enlightened self-interest – banks, insurance companies, or companies looking for sub-contractors have a direct interest in involvement with up and coming small firms – and has built up its budget out of its own enterprise to a turnover by 1989/90 of over £2 million a year. Greater Bristol Trust is by definition an agency for raising and passing through donations, but it also building itself an independent basis through endowment, at first on its own and now by the offer of one of the Charities Aid Foundation's major challenge grants.

A two-pronged approach to companies through systematic general marketing and also an individual and customised approach. Companies are individual cases, and by common consent involving them depends in the end on an individual approach geared to their own interests and potential. They have to be 'talked through', and this process puts heavy demands on staff time. There are other methods, notably the way in which Avon's Education-Industry Links unit mobilises the customers and brokers initiatives directly from schools to companies. The unit has also developed a network of district committees in cooperation with the CBI, and these are now being transformed into jointly chaired education-business partnerships serviced by the County Careers Service.

It is likely in many cases that the best use for additional funds available to agencies could well be rather modest additions to staff for making company contacts: GBT underlined the importance of being present and making contacts through a variety of networks. However, more formal methods are also useful. GBT also uses mailshots, as has Business in the Community in its campaign in the North West targeted on small and medium-sized companies. The Task Force built a data base of potential supporters and used a Ministerial visit to open a marketing campaign for a group of projects with worked-out business plans.

Reaching smaller companies is important for the development of private sector involvement on a large scale. Informants commented that small companies may have good reasons for limiting their community involvement: 'too busy cutting down the trees around them to think about planting new ones', or, as one medium-sized company itself said, 'we are too busy making money'. Agencies tend naturally to go first to the bigger companies, and, if they themselves are short of staff, they may not get much further.

However, smaller companies are being reached. The outstanding example is education-school links, in which around 6,000 businesses are involved. Avon claims nearly 100 per cent coverage of pupils for work experience, and probably 240 teacher placements in industry in 1990. BitC sees enterprise agencies as an effective vehicle for involving smaller firms: New Work Trust's 260 supporting businesses are not all large, and the emphasis on professional advice and business opportunities rather than demands for cash is attractive to many smaller firms. ARC Avon's new programme of short-term and part-time 'designated assignments' is beginning to reach solicitors and accountants. The Bristol Development Corporation has used Avon Valley Traders as a channel for involving local businesses in its projects for environmental and infrastructural improvement, as the Avon Education-Industry Links unit has used the Brislington Traders' association to strengthen its school-business network. GBT (like ARC Avon) is limited by the size of its staff, but is developing closer links with smaller as well as with large firms.

Staffing is a key factor, and the agencies operating in Bristol are very differently equipped. BDC, for example, is in a different league from ARC Avon, GBT, or TBI. For the smaller agencies, faced with what is a highly time-consuming task, a basic minimum of staff for marketing to the private sector is vital and not always achieved. We have no criticism of the competence of the people we have met in these agencies, but in some there are not enough of them, and sometimes without enough continuity. Secondees can and do fill the gap to some extent, but inevitably without the same degree of continuity as regular employees.

8.4 Overcoming constraints on good practice
Although companies' objectives and forms of contributing vary, the experience of the companies at which we have looked points to several general rules of good practice and ways of overcoming constraints identified by respondents.

Information about voluntary agencies
Companies themselves will choose in the end where they wish to be involved, but they need a range of choice among the needs and causes to which they might contribute. The companies which we interviewed are not uninformed givers – that is why they were selected – and a number of our company respondents were themselves very much part of the Bristol networks and well-informed about what was going on. Not all were, however. There was sometimes a certain vagueness about issues and agencies outside companies' immediate concern. The agencies promoting company involvement in Bristol are, as has been noted, building up a coherent strategy covering the main areas of the city's economic problems, but several company informants were still worried about the multiplicity and confusion of initiatives in Bristol. It is not enough for the agencies to be increasingly coherent among themselves. More effort is also needed to project a coherent picture back to companies, particularly those which are not themselves involved in the leading networks.

Apart from the GBT, however, networks in the voluntary sector tend to be weak. At the time of our study the Bristol Council for Voluntary Service was described as 'effectively non-existent'. A Bristol Community Groups Network was started in the early 1980s as a forum for the discussion and issues and for contact with the local authorities, but has no overall policy and little if any involvement with the private sector, and the Bristol Volunteer Bureau has done little as yet to promote volunteering from the workplace. There is scope here for closer cooperation between the existing umbrella groups and the GBT in providing information to businesses and to the partnership bodies about the needs of, and services provided by, community groups and voluntary bodies.

Company policies on community contributions
Clarity of criteria

With a dozen appeals a day and having to say 'no' to 99 per cent of them, as was said in IBM, you need to know what you are doing. Whatever a company's objectives, it is obviously important that they should be reflected in clear criteria for choosing between projects. Criteria in our companies varied from short and common-sensical, like those of Mosaic, to elaborate and sophisticated, like Lloyds' donations and sponsorship guidelines. One community body commented on the 'intuitive' nature of the contributions policies of many of its company supporters. It would be unreasonable, and a case of re-inventing the wheel, to expect all companies to work out such elaborate criteria on their own, and yet it could be helpful to them to have sharper standards and more detailed check-lists than at present. We hope that this and similar reports, and work on guidelines for policy by Business in the Community, will be of use in this respect.

In relation to the overall level of contributions, we noted wide variations and a need for a generally recognised 'yardstick'. This could be provided by a local Per Cent Club: Bristol and Avon should have one, linked to the Bristol Initiative and the Avon TEC.

Managing the local programme

Programmes can be run on a shoestring, but the string must not be too thin. Hewlett Packard felt that it was missing opportunities through not having a specific community affairs manager. Its Bristol plant, with 800 employees, was said to be reaching the point at which a specific job in that area could be carried: IBM, similarly, explained how a specific full time post for the South-West and Wales had emerged out of the experience of line managers in the region. Even full-time management needs support: IBM's manager had less opportunity than he would have wished to be 'pro-active', and one community relations manager had some four hundred applications a week passing over his desk and no supporting staff. Part-time management is inevitable in small companies and can be appropriate for local programmes in larger ones, and can be fully effective so long as jobs and relationships within the company are clearly defined: but again, as was said in Telecom Severnside, it can be 'stretched'.

One point to which staffing is particularly relevant is 'pro-activity': going out to look for the projects which will give the best value for money, as Telecom nationally and locally did when it launched its inner cities programme: and monitoring their progress, if only to avoid the occasional 'disaster'. It was clear that in some large companies which would like to be thoroughly 'pro-active' staffing was inadequate for this. and smaller companies cannot be expected to carry the staff which would allow them to be fully pro-active on their own. There are ways around this, for example Mosaic's use of GBT to suggest, assess, and monitor its charitable donations. Enterprise agencies, as was pointed out by BitC, can in their own field be very effective intermediaries; so can a network like that sponsored by Avon's EIL unit for school-business links. But some companies which might have been expected to use intermediaries did not do so to a significant extent.

We heard some strong comments about banks and other companies which 'dribble out' small cheques disproportionate to the scale of the cause to which they are contributing. In fact, as one manager at a national bank pointed out, 'dribbling' may be a reasonable strategy for the company's own purposes, and Sun Alliance made the point that small sums may go a long way, notably with youth organisations. However, Sun Life is an example of a company which has recently changed its policy to focus its grants and make them more worthwhile to receivers: about fifty charities in 1990 instead of 150 the year before.

Accounting and budgeting practices varied from precise to highly flexible. British Telecom made a significant point about the desirability of a rigorously defined budget. In Telecom accounting since privatisation is stricter – 'everything is costed out' – but for managing the community relations budget this was seen at national level as an advantage rather than a restriction. 'You have your budget and can do things', whereas previously, when costs tended to get lost, community affairs staff might have had to look around for a department with an unspent margin.

Company headquarters do not necessarily have much to say about their subsidiaries' programmes, and that is not necessarily a disadvantage. Allied Lyons leaves Harveys of Bristol to develop its own programme. Hewlett Packard has 'very little interplay' with its headquarters in Bracknell. But IBM and British Telecom are examples of the value which significant resources at HQ and a strong but flexible lead can have for local action. Telecom has a large-scale national programme of community involvement and effective and flexible interaction between its central units and its local managers. Flexibility in the relationship is a key point: we heard comments on the way in which over-formalisation and over-centralisation can either delay decisions or make a flexible response to local needs difficult.

Developing a coherent strategy among agencies

The agencies of development in Bristol do not form a systematic whole, and that is not surprising. They have grown up on the basis of initiatives from different sources and with different purposes in mind. There have been antagonisms to overcome: local government reorganisation in 1973/74, for example, left the City and the County at arm's length, and the City Council strongly resisted the introduction of the Bristol Development Corporation. BDC's forceful approach attracts double-edged comments: on the one hand that it 'has done more in one year than the local authorities in sixteen', but on the other that it is 'everyone's enemy'. There have been fears for traditional spheres of influence, and in Bristol, one informant said, 'you are in trouble if you pick up someone else's ball': the Chamber of Commerce at one stage feared a takeover by TBI and would have nothing to do with it. The newness of many agencies is itself a problem. Time is needed to develop their work and create a clear perception of it among other agencies. Some respondents took the view that agencies like TBI or the Task Force have still to 'prove themselves'.

Many informants found the variety of agencies and their unsystematic pattern bewildering, and some wondered whether coherence could ever be achieved. 'If you are looking for coherence', one manager said, 'you are spitting in the wind'. But coherence is in fact emerging in two main ways.

First, there is a convergence between the strategic visions of the main agencies on Bristol's economic development. 'Economic' should be stressed, for there is force in the argument of some voluntary organisations that social and community development has been put on the back burner. It has not been altogether forgotten, even by agencies which are primarily economic in orientation. The Development

Corporation, for example, has been in active dialogue with the voluntary organisations, has a clear conception of how its contributions to community development might be focussed for maximum effect, and has called in a consultant to help in framing its community policy. But even for BDC this has been a second stage of thinking: as was said in another agency, 'real wealth comes first'. There is a need to ensure that the social dimension receives higher priority and the moves in hand to form links between BDC and the voluntary sector are welcome; bodies such as GBT need to be brought into closer liaison with the TEC and BLT. The new BLT is also an appropriate vehicle for the development of more initiatives involving business as a partner in tackling social problems such as housing shortages. There could be scope for The Bristol Initiative BLT to develop a targeted 'spin-off' Business Support Group on the lines of the group formed in Moss Side (see Chapter 9) to work with the Task Force, Community Development Trust and enterprise agencies in the Task Force area. This kind of innovation would also help to raise the priority attached to social issues in urban renewal programmes in the city.

Second, there is increasing use of networking between agencies and awareness of how this can be organised. The development of close links between the TEC and the BLT for information exchange, 'signposting' for enquiries from companies and community bodies and coordination of initiatives, and the creation of network bodies affiliated to the TEC/BLT – such as a Bristol Per Cent Club and a local Common Purpose – would all assist this process. The Bristol Initiative, in bringing all the main local actors together and liaising well with the TEC, seems set to become a model of BLT development: together the BLT and TEC could emerge as the overall strategic forum for Bristol and Avon, bringing greater coherence after all to the local community investment scene.

8.5 Selected case studies
Mosaic Management Consulting Group
Mosaic is a management and organisational development consultancy founded in 1981 and established in Bristol in 1986. The company's business is about cultural change within organisations and includes promoting a 'values' approach among managers and staff in its client firms. It applies the same approach to itself ('we are our own first

customers'): the company has not only defined its own values but at the outset literally inscribed them on tablets of stone. Now after several years this set of corporate principles is in the process of being refined.

The company has 30 staff, a turnover in its last year of £2.1 million and pre-tax profits of £200,000, and is expanding rapidly. It contributes ten per cent of pre-tax profits to the community, an arbitrary figure but 'big enough to make a difference', whereas the Per Cent Club's standard of half of one per cent is regarded as 'not real'. Like many other small firms, Mosaic has found it a complicated business to give money away, but a chance meeting with the director of Greater Bristol Trust led to a good working arrangement. Eight per cent is covenanted through GBT on the basis that half this money goes to GBT's endowment, and is building within it a 'named fund' in the company's name, and the rest to projects proposed by GBT as within Mosaic's criteria: the company makes the final choice. Without GBT, it was pointed out, the company could not investigate projects properly, and even with GBT 'it is difficult'. The other two per cent is used for projects outside GBT's remit but of personal concern to staff and within their personal knowledge.

The company also allows five per cent of work time to be used for community activities. This is not compulsory, though in fact most join in, and the way in which time is used is at staff members' own discretion: but on the understanding that time taken is 'a proper part of the job' and must be used effectively, accounted for, and included in staff assessment. Staff members' use of community time is, incidentally, a way in which the company follows the progress of its projects.

Donations are decided and their progress logged, and use of community time accounted for, through a staff committee of five with a part-time secretary and the company chairman in the chair, meeting quarterly: but all staff members can attend quarterly meetings, and can put forward proposals for projects provided that they are in writing and for a specific amount. Once a project is agreed, members of staff who express an interest visit the body in question to find out more about the nature of the venture. In some cases this has led to a wish on the part of employees to help on a voluntary basis with the organisation concerned. The collective nature of employees' involvement should be underlined. There is a list of positive and negative criteria: a positive preference for local causes, those with staff involvement or connected to the company's work, and those where a grant has 'leverage': negative rules against party politics, direct action, 'not true to our values', profit-making activities, and causes which cannot attract other support. Appeals which arise out of cuts in government funding for public services may also be rejected.

The chief reason given for Mosaic's policy was 'a feeling of personal responsibility in the community' and the wish to put something back, but there is also at least one clear element of enlightened self-interest. In this company it is not public relations, for the company is not 'in it for publicity', though it may occasionally and accidentally get it or be developing what was called a 'hidden image': but it does have to do with the relation between performance and employees' morale and motivation. The first and last item on Mosaic's tablets of stone is that 'people and profits are of equal importance in our business', and the company's policies on community work and donations are part of a package which makes Mosaic an attractive place to work.

The ten per cent standard has been discussed and approved by the staff as a whole, even though it implies a cost for ordinary staff members as well as the major shareholders. Commitment to support on this scale, a member of the clerical staff said, is one of the things which attracts many of us to work here. Collective involvement and personal opportunity within the company's contribution policy help to bring the staff together, along with other features of the company's policy like its special version of single status, 'everyone carries boxes', meaning that the chairman too helps in carrying the paraphernalia of presentations around; and 'fun matters too', a half day a month for a staff meeting sometimes followed by sports and other social activities.

At the end of the day, as the tablets of stone say, 'everyone sells – our image and reputation are a result of everyone's pride in their job'. Profits count equally with people, and profitability makes generosity possible, but the company's community investment policy, through its effects on employee morale, is in turn one of the elements which underpin profitability.

Mosaic's directors are involved in local networks, like the Chamber of Commerce or the regional council of the CBI, and part of Mosaic's own business is to promote a 'values' approach among managers in its large network of client companies. These contacts have not so far been used to propagate the Mosaic message on community involvement, and there was some hesitation about how far to go in that direction. There could, it was said, be a danger of the preacher standing in the way of the message, and of doing good leading to being seen as a 'do-gooder'. Perhaps, it was suggested, the business schools should give the lead here. However, the possibility of moving quietly in that direction is on the company's agenda.

Applying the Mosaic model

Mosaic is clearly exceptional in many ways. Developing managers' perception of values happens to be its business, and it is not surprising that its perception of its own values is unusually explicit and coherent. Its level of community contribution, in terms of proportion of pre-tax profits, would for most other companies in Britain (though less so in America) be astonishing. Nevertheless, its experience serves to emphasise the fact that an enlightened approach to community investment and participation in policy development by staff is wholly compatible with good business sense: the benefits in terms of employee motivation and recruitment are evident. The level of community contributions achieved is remarkable, but underlines the scope that exists for many other firms, including small ones, to raise their percentage contributions. Finally, the existence of a coherent policy on community investment, which brings in all employees and forges a close and mutually beneficial link with a community agency, allows effective targeting of resources and informal monitoring of progress.

The Bristol Initiative (TBI)

TBI was formally constituted in March 1989 and its chief executive John Savage was appointed in April 1990. The Initiative is part of the growing network of business leadership teams inspired by the 1988 report from the CBI on Initiatives Beyond Charity. It emerged from discussions between the promotional agency Business in the Cities (now part of Business in the Community) and local bodies, notably the local authorities. A first general presentation of the new partnership was held in the summer of 1990, attracting senior company executives and heads of other organisations, as well as the local news media.

TBI is supported by a wide range of local companies and prominent individuals, and has succeeded in securing participation from all sectors in Bristol. Its directors are drawn from local companies, including branches of major national corporations, from the city and county authorities, the Employment Service, local business umbrella groups, higher education, the Bristol Development Corporation, and the Church. It has also formed links with the new Avon TEC.

TBI is conceived as a city-wide forum for strategic debate on regeneration ventures, identification of 'flagship' projects for public/private sector partnerships to follow up, 'catalysing' of partnerships between different bodies and sectors, and coordination of the many disparate initiatives which have grown up in recent years.

Among the projects which have been identified for action is the redevelopment of the Broadmead shopping centre with a view to enhancing the city's overall attractiveness to residents, employers and investors. In this the TBI's role is in coordinating the ideas of the local authority and the traders' association, helping raise finance and lobbying Government. A large increase in retailing jobs in Broadmead would directly benefit residents of inner city areas suffering higher than average unemployment rates. Another 'flagship' venture is to begin work on partnership projects in housing, an important local problem.

Messages on good practice for other Business Leadership Teams
Key aspects of TBI's approach to devising partnership projects are the need to avoid taking all the credit, so as to respect other bodies' need for recognition and 'ownership' of ventures, and to avoid 'mental indigestion' from trying to tackle too many large-scale projects at once.

The Bristol Initiative has overcome initial suspicions – common when BLTs are established – that it was attempting a 'takeover' of the role of existing bodies such as the Chamber of Commerce. The Chamber is now a close partner, and other bodies which have been suspicious of BLTs elsewhere have also joined the partnership – notably the local authorities. The importance of a diplomatic approach to other key local fora and networks needs to be borne in mind by all similar initiatives in the cities.

The selective approach to projects is one which will assist in the successful establishment of BLTs and similar ventures. Over-ambitious concentration on a number of big 'flagship' projects can lead not only to 'indigestion', as respondents noted, but also to scepticism and disappointment if progress is slow.

TBI also fills a real gap in the variety of Bristol partnerships and initiatives, rather than simply adding to the list of new ventures and competing for resources with them, as some other BLTs have done elsewhere. In Bristol there was a need for a high level strategic forum to coordinate discussion of infrastructural issues and social problems. With the Avon TEC handling training and enterprise projects, and TBI concentrating on flagship renewal projects and raising the priority given to social problems such as housing shortages, Bristol should be able to develop a well-coordinated system for strategic debate among all types of organisation involved in community regeneration and for exchange of information.

9 Case Study: Manchester

9.1 Introduction

Of the three case study cities, it is perhaps Manchester which displays the most remarkable contrasts between areas undergoing major urban renewal and those so far largely untouched by economic revival. The central area is being redeveloped through a number of large scale projects: it is planned that the G-Mex Exhibition Centre will be accompanied by a £30 million concert hall and office and housing development (the Great Bridgewater initiative); the Great Northern Warehouse is being turned into a festival marketplace; there has been substantial new office development; a light rail system is planned for the conurbation; and in Salford the creation of new housing, leisure and office facilities in the Quays is widely regarded as a highly successful example of property-led urban regeneration. Manchester has two Urban Development Corporations – one for central Manchester, set up in 1988, and one for the Trafford Park area, set up in 1987. Trafford Park DC is developing a large area of derelict former industrial estate for new offices and factories. The Central Manchester DC is developing office, reatil, leisure and housing space in a 470 acre site to the south and east of the city centre.

Alongside the notable developments in many parts of central Manchester, there are persistent and deep-rooted problems in other districts. Manchester contains classic inner city areas marked by high unemployment, very low levels of educational qualifications, industrial decline, racial discrimination, very poor quality housing and large numbers of especially disadvantaged residents, particularly lone parents. In Moss Side and Hulme, which has a government Task Force, unemployment is exceptionally high – some 32 per cent in Hulme and 22 per cent in Moss Side at the end of 1989; there is a weak economic base, with few significant local employers; and there is a severe problem of 'postcode discrimination' against recruitment of residents and investment from outside because of the area's reputation for social problems and crime. In East Manchester unemployment is also much higher than the city average: the district has lost much of its industrial base and has large areas of derelict land following plant closures.

The successes in renewal initiatives in the centre of Manchester could lead to the creation of thousands of new jobs; and many employers in the city have experienced shortages of staff. There should be considerable scope for equipping residents in the hard-hit inner city localities to take up new job opportunities in expanding sectors of the city's economy – for instance, in Trafford Park. Much of the most striking community involvement on the part of the private sector has been concerned with developing skills among the population of Moss Side and Hulme and East Manchester, as we shall see in this chapter. There is much good practice to be built upon in the 1990s, and there are good examples of the benefits of a long-term partnership approach by the private sector to areas with deep-seated economic and social problems.

For this case study we were referred to companies and other actors on the Manchester scene by senior staff at the government's Task Force in Moss Side and Hulme and at the government's City Action Team, which coordinates the activities of the Departments of Environment, Employment and Trade and Industry in the conurbation. Section 9.2 below examines some of the examples of direct private sector involvement with the community; section 9.3 looks at the operation of networks and partnership initiatives involving business; section 9.4 considers constraints on good practice identified by respondents. In section 9.5 there are detailed case studies of the Kellogg company's community involvement and of the Business Support Group established in Moss Side and Hulme.

9.2 Companies and their community links

As in the other cities visited, the major national corporations are active through their local organisations in the community in Manchester: familiar names such as Barclays, IBM, Laing and Marks & Spencer were frequently mentioned by respondents. In Manchester these are accompanied by major locally based employers with substantial community programmes – for example, Granada Television and Kellogg (see separate case study in section 9.5 below). The 'first division' of locally committed companies has developed effective partnership ventures, as described in section 9.3, as well as carrying out individual projects and policies for community support. Smaller firms in Manchester tend not to be integrated in the networks and partnerships involving the larger companies, but there are examples of effective involvement in the community, and Manchester Chamber of Commerce emphasises the contribution smaller firms make to its programmes for schools liaison.

Motivation for community investment
The range of reasons for involvement on the part of companies was wide. Many employers emphasised a desire to 'put something back into the community'; but many also recognised that a philanthropic approach was complemented by considerations of long-term and more immediate self-interest. The need to appeal to companies' sense of enlightened self-interest was stressed by public and voluntary sector agencies such as the Central Manchester Development Corporation (CMDC) and the City Action Team (CAT) and Task Force. Varying dimensions of self-interest were revealed:

- General concern for economic and social stability in Manchester and a desire to see the prosperity of the inner city areas increase in order to promote business. In the case of one company suffering from a serious problem of bad debts in inner city districts, one motivating factor was the desire to reduce their incidence through contributing to initiatives for training and enterprise support.
- Concern over recruitment of young people in the light of growing competition for school leavers and demographic trends reducing their numbers in coming years: this has led to interest in recruiting from groups which have been marginalised in the labour market – long-term unemployed people and inner city residents from ethnic minority communities. The need to match local people to local skills demand was a strong motivating force behind new initiatives in targeted recruitment, training and school-industry links.
- The scope for business development in community-oriented ventures: for instance, the construction firm Jarvis is involved in

publicly-funded training programmes through its own training company.

- The desire to gain local goodwill and ensure continuing support from the local community : this was part of the motivation for involvement for Clayton Aniline, a chemicals firm situated next to a residential area of East Manchester; and for Granada Television, the renewal of whose broadcasting contract depends in part on its image and record as a contributor to the community in Manchester and the North West region.
- The desire to raise the profile of the company was the key factor behind sponsorship schemes; in other areas of activity securing publicity tended not to be a strong motivating force.

Policy and budgets

The local operations of the major corporate donors worked within the policy framework laid down at national level; among locally headquartered firms, the large ones such as Granada and Kellogg ran comprehensive programmes for community involvement with specialist staff and a broad range of activities. Other firms, especially smaller ones, tended not to have formalised policies on community involvement and instead to operate budgets for charitable donations and sponsorship, or to react in a largely ad hoc manner to requests for support. In one case a local small firm was much constrained by guidelines laid down by the head office of its parent company.

Most companies contacted had a donations budget for local requests for financial support: generally these budgets were very small (up to £10,000 only) in relation both to the scale of local needs and to sums spent on national sponsorship programmes by some firms. One respondent noted the enormous difference between his local budget for community contributions in an inner city area (£5,000) and his group's national budget for sponsorship, which was over one hundred times larger; he argued that a transfer of some resources from national promotions to locally targeted economic and social regeneration would not only be of long-term benefit to the community but could also generate publicity and public goodwill just as effectively as sponsorship schemes did.

The problem of securing more local resources for companies to spend and of obtaining a higher level of local awareness among firms aroused strong feelings among some respondents. There was severe criticism of the 'London-centred' perspective of many national companies and of the lack of autonomy and resources allocated to local branches. IBM and Marks & Spencer were identified as cases of good practice in this respect, but other big firms were criticised for laying down inflexible policies at national level. As one chief executive put it, 'No-one on London knows how to press a button in Manchester to make things happen'.

Types of community links

Respondents in companies, public bodies and voluntary agencies agreed that there was now a widespread movement in firms' community policies away from concentration on charitable donations towards a greater emphasis on proactive involvement with community groups and networks, and towards seeing staff time and expertise as the major contribution which the private sector can make. Respondents from public agencies and community bodies agreed that provision of expert advice and of secondees or board members for new ventures could be more significant than financial support.

Examples of the types of community links encountered are given below.

Donations

All companies contacted made donations in cash or kind or both to community groups, charities or schools. There were interesting examples of imaginative good practice, as with Granada's establishment of an Actors' Centre on its premises, providing free accomodation, and Royal Mail's donation of computers plus installation and training to the new Community Development Trust in Moss Side and Hulme.

Education and training

Education and training are regarded as a priority by companies involved in community investment and by community groups. There was a strong emphasis among companies of all sizes that the main need in the inner city areas, especially Moss Side and Hulme, was to equip the local population with marketable skills and qualifications, in order to boost their chances of obtaining jobs in areas such as Trafford Park and to attract more businesses into these districts. Small firms in the inner city saw their main contribution to the community as simply being there to provide a limited number of jobs and thus contribute to the local economy.

A number of companies are involved in school-industry links and Compact schemes, with work experience for students and placements for schoolteachers. This is an area of activity important to the small firms contacted, and to large employers such as Scottish and Newcastle Breweries, whose local community contributions in Manchester are focussed on school links and support for young people.

Recruitment initiatives

The policy of local recruitment and provision of customised training had become important in a number of companies, motivated as noted above by anxieties over demographic trends in relation to recruitment as well as concern over the disadvantages suffered by inner city districts. Smaller firms such as Dawnvale in East Manchester and LT Switchgear in Moss Side recruit locally in any case, but have been involved in schemes for improving local opportunities: for instance, Dawnvale has worked with the City Action Team on a job interview guarantee programme for local people. A notable case of success in local recruitment and targeting is provided by Scottish and Newcastle Breweries, which was obliged by the city council to take on local people for semi-skilled jobs when they sought to expand their Moss Side site, which involved demolishing council flats. The deal struck involved local recruitment and contribution to re-housing costs. Previously the company had employed few local people; the initiative proved to be a major success, and there were some 4,000 applications for 100 jobs under an interview guarantee scheme. The benefits were significant, both for the district and for the company:

- the firm revised its selection procedures for recruitment and came up with a sophisticated new system of assessment for recruitment and for training, in which applicants' potential was taken into account rather than existing qualifications and work achievement;
- the local recruits proved to be of good quality;
- a new pool of labour was opened up;
- the long-term unemployed recruits were very highly motivated;
- turnover of staff from the local recruits was low.

This is a good example of 'tactical' self-interest considerations leading a company to a more 'enlightened' strategic view of the potential of mainstream company activity to contribute to community support. Moreover, the radical overhaul of the firm's selection procedures which followed its agreement to recruit long-term unemployed people has brought 'community investment' considerations into the heart of its personnel policy.

A similar case is that of Jarvis Training Management, which operates publicly-funded training schemes in construction and has targeted the long-term unemployed as a recruitment pool. The 'tactical' interest is in the opportunity to run a profitable training operation as well as help the unemployed; the more strategic element is apparent in the company's involvement in partnerships with public sector agencies and its contribution to the Manchester TEC, and its recognition of the community goodwill which can result from 'enlightened' activities. Both Jarvis and Scottish & Newcastle Breweries illustrate how short-term considerations can provide a point of entry to a longer range commitment to adapting mainstream activities to community needs.

Other Joblink schemes have had a chequered history in the inner city areas but are now being developed for Moss Side and Hulme with the support of a range of companies (see sections 9.3 and 9.5).

Secondments and other assignments
Provision of staff time and expertise was highly valued by community groups and by public agencies such as the Task Force. However, secondments were not widely available – even the most committed local companies said that they had no spare staff, having developed 'lean' workforces during the 1980s – and were largely the preserve of major corporations such as Barclays and Marks & Spencer. A further problem with secondments was the quality of personnel provided: there were anxieties among some community respondents that secondees might be 'charity cast-offs' near retirement, when what was needed were mid-career managers of high calibre. An example of good practice commended by community informants was Barclays' secondment of a manager to the enterprise agency AED in Moss Side and Hulme, and the manager's subsequent take-up of a place on the AED board.

Short-term or part-time assignments of managers can also be highly valuable in injecting business knowledge into voluntary bodies and enterprise agencies, and in supplying expertise to partnership bodies. A number of companies were supplying managers to bodies such as the TEC and the North West Business Leadership Team (BLT), or staff to sit on boards and committees of schools and colleges. Provision of business expertise is also the key element in the assistance provided by the Business Support Group in Moss Side and Hulme (see section 9.5).

Sponsorship
Several firms were involved in arts and social sponsorship in the locality, although in general the main sponsorship budgets were national ones.

Important as examples of individual companies' community links are, the most significant activity in Manchester involves business contributions to partnerships and networks. These are examined in the next section.

9.3 Partnerships and networks
Manchester, like Birmingham and Bristol and several other cities in recent years, has seen the development of a multitude of partnerships, new initiatives for enterprise promotion and urban renewal, and networks involving the private sector. We list here the main multi-firm groupings and some significant partnerships linking the private, public and voluntary sectors.

Multi-firm groupings
The Chamber of Commerce
Manchester has a large Chamber of Commerce which has a major role in numerous local ventures. The Chamber has some 3,000 member companies which pay a voluntary subscription to support collective activity. Among its activities relevant to community involvement are:
- establishment of the enterprise agency Manchester Business Venture, sponsored by some forty companies;
- overall responsibility for the enterprise agency Tameside Business Advice Service;
- establishment of Network Manchester, a local employers' network for coordination of training provision;
- delivery of youth training and ET schemes;
- school-industry compacts focussed on inner city schools;

- an Education Liaison Unit to coordinate work experience schemes, teacher placements and other ventures linking business and education;
- involvement in multi-sector partnership initiatives such as the TEC, a European Information Centre and the East Manchester Initiative.

Business Support Group for Moss Side and Hulme

The latest multi-firm group to emerge is the Business Support Group (BSG), established on the initiative of Kellogg in 1989 with the help of Business in the Community. The BSG is a partnership of local companies which aims to catalyse and coordinate private sector activity in Moss Side and Hulme, working alongside community bodies and public agencies. It is a local spin-off from the Business Leadership Team (BLT) established for the North West region. The BSG is described in detail in a separate case study in section 9.5 below.

Trafford Park

The Trafford Park development area has an informal 'Major Manufacturers Group' chaired by a Kellogg manager and an industrial council, TRAFIC.

Multi-sector partnerships

There are many ventures involving some form of partnership between different sectors in Manchester. The main actors and initiatives are outlined below.

Manchester Training and Enterprise Council

The new Manchester TEC became fully operational in December 1990. Its board and specialist committees bring together representatives of individual companies, the Chamber of Commerce, higher education, trade unions, the city council, Development Corporations, public agencies and the voluntary sector. The inner city areas are represented through members such as the Moss Side enterprise agency AED, companies from the Business Support Group and the Moss Side and District Tenants' Association. The TEC has four area groups and five special committees (for vocational and youth training, adult unemployed training, enterprise, training for the employed, and equal opportunities).

Central Manchester Development Corporation
The Central Manchester Development Corporation has established
links with the Chamber, City Council, TEC and the City Action Team
for partnership in various projects. An Employment Consultancy
Service has been set up with the CAT, City Council and TEC in order
to simplify provision of advcie and information to small firms: the aim
is to help small businesses through what one respondent called a
'maze' of networks and advisory bodies and help firms get the most
out of the range of public schemes and grants available. The CMDC
has worked with the British Council on the relocation of the latter's
headquarters to Manchester, which should create some 500 new jobs;
partnership initiatives are being sought to provide training for inner
city residents in order to enable them to fill the jobs. CMDC is also
involved in various education link schemes.

Manchester City Council
The City Council has been strongly opposed to the establishment of
the Development Corporations, but has recently adopted a pragmatic
approach to the existence of the CMDC; various partnership ventures
are in process with the CMDC and the private sector in the city centre.
Similar collaborations have been successful in Salford between the
Salford Council and the private sector in the development of the Quays
area. The Manchester City Council is represented on the area groups
and delivery committees of the TEC, on the Moss Side and Hulme
Community Development Trust, and is a partner of the Chamber of
Commerce in a new initiative for coordination of employment and
enterprise projects in East Manchester.

Business Leadership Team
A number of leading firms are members of the North West Business
Leadership Team (BLT), which has so far concentrated on marketing
the region and on lobbying for infrastructural improvements for the
whole region (such as road improvements). The Business Support
Group in Moss Side and Hulme is linked to the BLT.

City Action Team and Task Force
Numerous partnership ventures involve the City Action Team and the
Moss Side and Hulme Task Force. The Task Force is working with
the Business Support Group and the Moss Side Enterprise Agency

AED; it has also fostered the new community forum for Moss Side, the Community Development Trust, which brings together representatives of community groups, public bodies and the private sector to plan for local initiatives and provide a focal point for discussion. The City Action Team has worked in partnership with Jarvis Training Management Ltd. on a Home Safety Scheme for East Manchester, which provides a free advice service to households on home safety, security and energy saving.

The Flying Start initiative
Over the past eight years Granada Television and private and public sector partners have sponsored an enterprise competition, 'Flying Start', for small firms located in (or prepared to locate in) the North West. Awards of up to £40,000 are made from a trust fund, plus training through the Business Development Unit of Manchester Business School. The scheme includes production of an excellent information booklet for small firms, giving contact details for all private and public sector agencies offering advice and assistance to companies. This is good practice which deserves emulation elsewhere, particularly in view of the proliferation and complexity of services available to the small firms sector.

9.4 Overcoming constraints on good practice
As in Birmingham and Bristol, there are impressive new developments in Manchester and a ferment of new activity involving the private sector in community action. The partnership approach is well established in the city and there is agreement that progress is being amde on a number of fronts in urban renewal. However, there is also wide agreement on a number of problems which place constraints on further development of good practice by the private sector and others in community investment. These obstacles are discussed briefly in this section.

Government funding and policy
As we found elsewhere, respondents from companies and community groups complained about the problems they associated with working with government agencies. There was confusion over the funding system for inner city initiatives and the number of different programmes in urban policy; two senior managers argued for direct

Treasury funding to overcome problems caused by fragmentation of programme funding between departments; there were complaints over what were seen as 'jealousies and in-fighting' between departments and agencies; the lack of core funding and emphasis on project funding were criticised as an example of short-term thinking in a policy area which demanded long-term strategy and risk taking on the part of the public sector as well as business; and there was strong criticism of what was seen as the constant changing of policies and rules in urban programmes, which made it hard for the private sector to plan ahead. These are familiar points by now; the vigour with which they are made must be taken into account if government wishes to maximise the cooperation of the private sector in urban renewal and community investment.

The role of the local authorities

A further area of political problems is the relationship between Government and local authorities. In Manchester there has been a history of abortive initiatives in fields such as training because of disputes between the City Council and government over the Employment Training scheme and the imposition of the Development Corporations. Such disputes have a discouraging effect on many companies which are seeking a way into partnership ventures. However, there are positive developments to report, in that the City Council has taken a more pragmatic line on collaboration with CMDC recently and is involved in the Manchester TEC. The Council has also become fully involved in the Community Development Trust in Moss Side and Hulme (see section 9.5).

'Cultural' differences in the community

Another factor in the history of failed initiatives in areas such as Moss Side is the 'cultural gap', as one respondent put it, between the private sector and local community groups, which are likely to be hostile to or at least suspicious of business and public sector interest after years of being left on the margins of the Manchester economy. There are no short cuts to partnership between private, public and community bodies in such cases, and this is fully recognised by Kellogg and its partners in the Business Support Group in Moss Side (see section 9.5). The development of renewal projects in inner city districts will need patience, willingness to experiment and fail, long-term commitment and above all dialogue with the community rather than imposition of 'solutions'.

Although it is too early to judge the success of the BSG in Moss Side and the new Community Development Trust, the experience to date is widely regarded as encouraging and respondents from all sectors said that there is a genuine sense of trust and partnership emerging after initial suspicion from the multiplicity of community groups as to the motives of the private sector partners and the Task Force. The Moss Side area now has a Business Support Group which connects the area to wider company networks; an enterprise agency backed by major firms; and a Community Development Trust to provide a forum for discussion and coordination between all partners in the area. This 'triad' seems to be highly promising and an effective model for other 'problem areas'. East Manchester needs a similarly coherent approach by partnership bodies: it has a Community Forum which could develop into a focus for coordination and debate as in Moss Side; there is an initiative for economic strategy for the area involving the Chamber of Commerce and the City Council; it now needs to draw in private sector support, and the creation of a Business Support Group for the area deserves to be considered in the light of the Moss Side experience.

Such initiatives involving the community groups fully in partnership would also help to place social regeneration issues higher up the agenda for urban renewal in the city; as in our other cities, the emphasis has been on property-led development to date and there is a lot to do in tackling the social problems which persist in the inner city areas. The establishment of Community Development Trusts as in Moss Side can provide a focus for what is often a highly fragmented set of community groups and voluntary bodies.

Getting more companies involved

Some respondents noted that the same business leaders tend to appear on most of the partnership boards and committees. This is useful in that it reinforces networking, but is not healthy in the long run if it indicates that a new generation of leaders is not coming forward or that the culture of corporate investment in the community is not attracting new firms. In particular small and medium firms tend not to be invited into networks and partnerships, and more effort should go into drawing them in: the TEC may well be successful in this respect and the BSG model could accommodate small firms as well as large employers. Recruitment of new leaders and new companies could be assisted by establishment of a Common Purpose scheme for Manchester, and of a local Per Cent Club; both could be affiliated to the TEC to ensure integration into the mainstream local business networks.

Coordination and information

As in the other cities, respondents from all sectors bemoaned what they saw as the chaotic proliferation of initiatives in recent years in the city and the absence of a city-wide forum to 'pull it all together'. One civil servant wondered how any firms found their way through the 'maze' of business advice services; a chief executive estimated that there were some 80 sources of funding for different forms of urban regeneration in Manchester, and said that TEC member firms were 'bewildered and horrified' by the number of new organisations set up locally in recent years. The last thing needed was more networks, he thought. Others expressed puzzlement over the North West Business Leadership Team, seen as a 'mysterious' or 'remote' body with no clear role.

To some extent the confusions over lack of coordination of activities and information flows are inevitable given the newness of many ventures, such as the TEC, BSG and the Development Corporation. However, there are mixed views over the need for an overall strategic forum that can act as a lead body for referring enquiries in relation to business action in the community, whether from firms or from voluntary groups; that can pull together information sources (the CMDC's initiative on employment consultancy with the TEC and CAT is a promising development in this respect); and that can address itself to the full range of regeneration issues, social as well as infrastructural and economic. Some see a gap needing to be filled by a strategic forum; but we have also heard the strongly expressed view that yet another body – for instance a Manchester Business Leadership Team – would simply 'get people's backs up' and compete with existing bodies and the informal networks which bring all the private and public sectors leaders together.

If there is a gap, it has been filled in part at least by the TEC, which has involved all relevant sectors. There may be a case for providing a more formalised occasional forum for representatives from the

Chamber, TEC, individual firms, higher education, voluntary sector, City Council and Development Corporations to discuss issues not covered by the TEC – principally infrastructural issues and social regeneration initiatives relating to the inner city areas. Given the effective informal networking which appears to take place already and the existence of a regional BLT for the North West, it is unlikely that there is any place for a Manchester BLT on the model of the Bristol Initiative (see section 7.5 above), which would compete for resources and ownership of projects. However, a more formalised system for meetings of key local actors on infrastructural and social questions in which there is common interest may be useful. This could provide a clear focus for businesses and other groups and could simplify the city's networking and information flows in relation to partnership initiatives.

9.5 Selected case studies
The Kellogg Company

Kellogg has had its UK headquarters in Trafford Park for half a century, and is a major employer in Manchester. The company has developed a substantial programme of community investment over the last ten years and is now widely regarded as a example of good practice by other companies and agencies from the public and voluntary sector in the city.

Before the early 1980s the company's level of community activity was relatively low: there was a charitable donations budget of around £10,000 in 1980. The impetus for change came in the early 1980s from the then Chairman and Company Secretary. The decision was made to increase the level of donations and to develop a policy for community investment in order to target resources effectively and set priorities among the enormous number of requests for support received. Other factors in the growth of Kellogg's programme were desire for long-term revival of the inner city economy; concern over the effect on the workforce of working in a depressed area; and concern over the physical and economic decline of inner city areas in the early 1980s recession, in particular of Trafford Park itself: heavy industry declined, many jobs were lost and large areas of land fell into dereliction.

Policy has developed considerably over the past decade. The company's aim to be a 'socially responsible' corporate citizen is set out in a Mission Statement prepared in the early 1980s, and the range of activities in which the firm is involved has expanded. There has been a shift from an emphasis on charitable donations to community investment in a broad sense, and the budget for community support has grown very substantially. The budget for UK community investment in 1990 was around £610,000, representing 1 per cent of pre-tax profits (Kellogg was a founder member of the national Per Cent Club). In 1989 over 300 charitable donations were made amounting to £345,000; additional spending on other forms of community investment brought the total expenditure to £574,000.

Policy is implemented by the Corporate Affairs department, which also embraces government relations and public affairs. There is a 'donations committee' which is chaired by the manager of Corporate Affairs, who processes requests for support. Increasingly, the policy is to target resources on 'community economic regeneration' within the North West generally and the inner city in Manchester in particular. There is also an emphasis on welfare, education, health and environmental regeneration. Some two-thirds of total community support is focussed on the North West, with the remainder spread nationwide. Setting priorities is crucial: 'It is very easy to give money away; it is more difficult to make it truly effective'. The guiding strategy in relation to inner city renewal in Manchester is to help develop new economic opportunities in areas such as Trafford Park and equip unemployed residents of districts such as Moss Side and Hulme to take up new jobs created by revival and by demographic pressures on employers. A key element of the overall approach is to seek partners from the private and public sector ('two plus two can equal five') and to work in collaboration with community groups, not impose solutions.

Forms of community involvement other than donations include:
- partnership with private and public sector bodies in the regeneration of Trafford Park, and a leading role in the area's Major Manufacturers' Group and Industrial Council (TRAFIC);
- provision of facilities (for example, hosting of an annual Wheelchair Marathon around Trafford Park);
- involvement in school-industry links, for example local COMPACT schemes, short placements for teachers, provision of time for employees to serve as school governors;

- work experience placements and chairing Fullemploy Group's local board in the Manchester area;
- involvement of staff on boards of enterprise agencies (for instance in Moss Side), the Manchester TEC, local and regional business groupings and voluntary agencies;
- a leading role in the Moss Side and Hulme Business Support Group (see below) and in various initiatives in the district, such as investment with the Task Force in a new grocery store for Hulme;
- matching of funds raised by employees for charitable causes.

Full-time secondments are not provided, since the workforce is kept 'lean'. Local suppliers are welcomed but there is no formal policy on local purchasing within the overall framework for community involvement.

Messages on good practice
Kellogg's role in Moss Side and Hulme goes back to 1985 when it was involved in development of the Fullemploy initiative in the area. There have been many difficulties in achieving mutual understanding with community groups in the district, but since 1989 there seems to have been significant progress with the setting up of the Business Support Group under Kellogg's leadership and the development of the local Community Development Trust. The involvement of Kellogg in Moss Side and Hulme is a good example of how a company can make a significant contribution to renewal in a highly disadvantaged area through a long-term commitment to support, partnership with public agencies, a catalytic role in bringing in other firms, and dialogue with members of the local community. The company's experience also shows how firms can build up programmes for community investment from a low base, given commitment from senior management and a clear policy framework for setting priorities for action and targeting local needs.

Moss Side and Hulme Business Support Group (BSG)
As noted above, Moss Side and Hulme is a severely disadvantaged area of the Manchester inner city, with very high levels of unemployment, especially among the young black population, poor housing, low skill levels and many other social problems. For years the area has been on the margins of the Manchester economy and has been starved of private sector interest and investment, with a few

exceptions such as Scottish and Newcastle Breweries' development in the centre of the district. During the 1980s there were several largely unsuccessful attempts to get companies and voluntary agencies involved in the area: these foundered because of poor communications, lack of adequate resources and commitment to long-term action, fragmentation among community groups, and suspicion and hostility among community bodies towards private sector companies which hitherto had shown no interest in the district. In the late 1980s the area was given a government Task Force, which also encountered many of these difficulties.

Following the successes in renewal of the Trafford Park area, in which it had been closely involved, the Kellogg Company, which had previously been active independently in Moss Side, decided to take the lead in setting up a partnership venture in the district which would provide some coordinated activity between the private and public sectors. In 1989 Kellogg, assisted by Business in the Community, established the BSG as a spin-off from the North West Business Leadership Team. Leading locally based companies were approached and there are now 13 members:

Kellogg; British Telecom; Barclays Bank; Co-operative Bank; Laing North West; Price Waterhouse; 3M; Whitbread; Royal Mail; Norweb; Royal Brewery; Amec ; and Manchester Business School.

The BSG was launched by the Prince of Wales in Moss Side in September 1989. The aims of the BSG are set out in its Initial Charter (see below). The group seeks to focus private sector support for the regeneration of the area, work in partnership with public agencies and the community, and work to improve the employment prospects of residents. The companies involved all see their participation not only in terms of social responsibility but also in terms of long range benefits to their businesses from increased prosperity, social stability and recruitment potential. The support to be provided includes professional expertise and advice, secondments, equipment and furniture, loans, sponsorship, access to facilities and training ventures such as customised programmes. Three BSG members are on the board of the local enterprise agency AED, which focusses especially on the ethnic minority communities in the area.

A key element in the BSG's approach is the emphasis on partnership. The BSG's first concrete venture has been to work with the Task Force, Business in the Community and local community groups to set up a new Community Development Trust (CDT). This was established in 1989, with core funding from the Task Force, and is now chaired by a member of the local community. The aim of the CDT is to provide a forum for discussion between all parties on initiatives for regeneration, and to bring disparate community groups together. There are four private sector trustees from the BSG firms, who sit alongside eight trustees elected from the local community; and there are two members from the City Council. The CDT should prove to be the focus for liaison between the district and outside bodies such as the TEC and Central Manchester and Trafford Park Development Corporations, and is now seeking to identify projects for private sector involvement in fields such as job links, priority hiring, customised training and transfer of management skills. BSG members are contributing time and resources to assist the development of the CDT – for instance in provision of computer equipment and training in its use, accountancy advice, selection of staff, consultancy on business planning and advice on management. They also participate in CDT initiatives such as job interview guarantee schemes and customised training projects, and have a key role as catalysts in attracting further business support.

In addition to their support for the CDT, members of the BSG have raised significant private sector cash contributions to supplement public grants towards the capital costs of refurbishing a listed building on the border of Hulme and Moss Side. This building is to become the Nia Centre for African and Caribbean Culture in the North West, owned by the local community. The members of the BSG see this centre as 'a vital catalyst in changing the image of the area, crucial to sustainable economic and social regeneration'.

Messages on good practice
Although there have been many problems on the way to establishing the BSG and the CDT, and although it is obviously too early to gauge the success of the ventures, respondents from all parties agree that the BSG and its support for the Trust are among the most promising developments on the urban renewal scene in Manchester. The companies involved have committed themselves to a partnership approach and to long-term action, and have evidently succeeded in overcoming much of the inevitable initial suspicion and scepticism which met the new venture. The BSG appears to work effectively in

harnessing the specific skills and expertise of member firms for supporting the CDT. The combination of a business support group, which links the community to wider business networks, and a community development trust, which acts as a partnership forum for private, public and above all community participants, would seem to be a model worth emulating elsewhere in Manchester (for instance in East Manchester) and in inner city districts in other parts of the country. Finally, the partnership approach and the development of a charter for the BSG (see below) have contributed to the integration of community investment in the member firms' mainstream business.

Moss Side and Hulme Business Support Group – Charter

In October 1989 the Group adopted the following Charter which sets out its objectives:

The aim is to assist in the economic and social regeneration of the Moss Side and Hulme and immediately surrounding areas of Manchester. To do this the Business Support Group (BSG) will:

1. work in partnership with any other agencies or organisations committed to the regeneration of the area. However, it will remain independent of any one interest group and will set its own priorities and targets;

2. assist, where possible, in the analysis of problems and opportunities in the area and in the development of strategies to tackle these issues;

3. encourage and assist in the growth of existing and new economic development initiatives in the area by providing support such as professional expertise and advice, equipment, secondees, finance, sponsorship, access to facilities, premises and any other available and appropriate means. In particular, it will seek to support long-term, income generating initiatives;

4. seek to increase employment opportunities for residents of the area, e.g. through targeted recruitment, 'open door' employment policies, support for and provision of training;

---

5. support the development of enterprise in the area, e.g. through local purchasing, soft loans, support for business advice agencies, provision of workspace;

6. seek to improve the image of the area within the business community in Greater Manchester and other areas;

7. encourage investment in the area and seek to attract new resources to the area in support of the regeneration effort;

8. at all times seek to work in cooperation with residents of the area;

9. maintain an overview of business involvement in the area, help advise other companies on effective ways to become involved in the area and act as a focus for other bodies seeking private sector support.

To achieve these objectives, member companies will:

1. endorse the aims and objectives of the BSG at the most senior level within the company;

2. establish a Working Group of senior individuals which will undertake the necessary actions in pursuit of their objectives;

3. make a commitment of resources to be deployed in pursuit of the objectives;

4. meet 4 times a year, or more frequently if necessary, to review progress and agree a strategy for future action;

5. seek to develop and implement a long-term rolling strategy for the regeneration of the area in partnership with the community and the public sector.

Caring for communities: why companies get involved

Communities sustain business by providing employees, customers and suppliers. Therefore, if business is to be successful, companies must have a vested interest in encouraging the economic and social vitality of the communities in which they operate.

The members of the Moss Side and Hulme Business Support Group wish to participate in and contribute towards the economic and social regeneration of the area, not only as an expression of altruism, but also because they recognise that community involvement benefits business in many important ways.

Active involvement with education and training programmes helps companies develop a quality, skilled local workforce as well as improving job prospects for unemployed people, members of minority ethnic groups and women.

- Supporting the growth of small and developing businesses benefits the entire commercial sector by stimulating local market growth, widening the supplier base, attracting new investments and increasing social stability.

- Creating goodwill for companies among employees, customers, shareholders, legislators and influential opinion-formers.

By formalising their commitment in mission statements and boardroom policies supported by senior management, members of the Business Support Group have ensured that community involvement is a central feature of their mainstream business activity. These business leaders recognise that supporting economic regeneration is a fundamental prerequisite for sustained commercial success in the 1990s.

Taking action on community investment

This section is aimed at senior managers in companies that wish to become involved in community investment. It is intended as a general set of guidelines to encourage them to think about their aims and help them frame their companies' policies.

Aims and objectives
Guidelines for action
- analysis of the company's aims in relation to investment in the community in terms of long- and short-term benefits to both company and community;
- development of criteria for assessing whether or not objectives have been met and of a system of periodic review of aims;
- publication of aims, objectives and benefits to employees, shareholders and community organisations (possibly including preparation of a 'mission statement').

Development of corporate policy
Guidelines for action
- development of written guidelines on policy for community investment and budgetary allocation, aimed at employees, shareholders and community organisations. The guidelines will set out the basis of allocations, priority areas, national/local emphasis and include guidelines for policy review;
- institution of procedures to ensure accurate reporting of all resources devoted to community investment – donations, sponsorship, allocations of staff time and other resources;
- publication of details of expenditure and activities in annual reports or special documents on community action.

Activities in the community
Guidelines for action
- examination of the scope for employee volunteering and matching support for employees' fund-raising activities;

- review of the scope for activities, such as local purchasing from small firms; investment in inner city areas; environmental improvement schemes; targeted recruitment and training schemes; school-industry links; membership of local representative bodies such as the Chamber of Commerce; secondments and other forms of staff assignment to community bodies;
- institution of procedures for regular reviews of community activities.

Organisation for community investment
Guidelines for action
- establishment of a distinct community investment department or identification of a manager for community investment to report to the company board, with clear guidelines on the relationships between community investment, personnel and purchasing;
- clear allocation of responsibilities and budgets to managers involved in making donations, organising sponsorships and forming other links with community bodies;
- training for managers responsible for community links (and for other staff), including guidance on the nature and extent of their discretion to initiate effective partnerships with community organisations; and on how to evaluate the success of activities, if necessary taking independent advice on policy implementation and organisation;
- development of policies on the allocation of resources between company headquarters and local branches, including consideration of the scope for increased devolution of resources to allow more targeting on local problems;
- involvement of employees in deciding priorities for company action.

Partnerships and networks
Guidelines for action
- contact national and local voluntary agencies for information on partnership activities;
- contact local business associations and private/public sector partnership bodies for information on multi-firm and multi-sector initiatives in the community;
- publicise community investment ideas to customers and suppliers;
- join national or local organisations such as Business in the Community and the Per Cent Club.

Appendix 2

A guide to information sources

Contacts for different community activities

This section indicates organisations at national and local level that can help companies in developing their policies in particular areas of community investment. Addresses are given in the directory that follows.

Financial support and gifts in kind

Companies can help voluntary bodies and community groups through cash donations and long term financial support, and through in-kind contributions such as donation of goods and facilities.

National contacts

Action Resource Centre; Business in the Community; Charities Aid Foundation; Directory of Social Change; National Council for Voluntary Organisations; the Per Cent Club.

Local contacts

Action Resource Centre regional offices; Business in the Community regional offices; Community Trusts; Councils for Voluntary Service.

Sponsorship of community initiatives and events

Companies can sponsor social and environmental projects as well as sporting and arts events.

National contacts

Action Match (social sponsorship); Business in the Community (Business in the Environment target team); Groundwork Foundation (environmental projects).

Local contacts

Action Match regional offices; local Groundwork Trusts.

Secondments and volunteering

Companies can support voluntary and public organisations through secondment of staff on a full-time or part-time basis over long-term or short-term assignments. Related forms of community involvement are volunteering by employees in local organisations and assignment of senior staff to the boards of schools, Chambers of Commerce, enterprise agencies, Training and Enterprise Councils (TECs; LECs in Scotland) and other bodies.

National contacts
Action Resource Centre (secondment); Business in the Community; Volunteer Centre (employee volunteering); Volunteers.

Local contacts
Action Resource Centre regional offices; Chambers of Commerce; enterprise agencies; schools, colleges and education authorities; the Government's City Action Teams and inner city Task Forces; TECs and LECs; local Volunteer Bureaux.

Provision of training and expertise
Companies can offer management advice, training courses and technical expertise to voluntary bodies and community groups.

National contacts
Action Resource Centre; Business in the Community; the Industrial Society; National Council for Voluntary Organisations.

Local contacts
Action Resource Centre regional offices; Chambers of Commerce; Councils for Voluntary Service; enterprise agencies; the Government's City Action Teams and inner city Task Forces.

Industry/education links
Companies can form close working links with schools, colleges, polytechnics and universities. School links can involve Compact schemes, work experience initiatives, company visits, teacher placements, management advice and training schemes.

National contacts
Council for Industry and Higher Education; Confederation of British Industry; the Industrial Society.

Local contacts
Chambers of Commerce; local education authorities; schools, colleges and higher education bodies; TECs and LECs.

Training and employment initiatives
Companies can implement policies for targeted recruitment from specific groups in the local community; for customised training courses for specific jobs and groups in the community; and for participation in public training schemes.

National contacts
Business in the Community; Employment Department; Fullemploy Group; the Industrial Society; Institute of Personnel Management.

Local contacts
Chambers of Commerce; the Government's City Action Teams and inner city Task Forces; TECs and LECs; Employment Service Jobcentres.

Support for local enterprise
Companies can promote local enterprise by implementing policies for increased local purchasing and recruitment; by supporting local enterprise agencies and start-up firms; through involvement in local economic development initiatives – for instance via Chambers of Commerce; and by sponsoring managed workspaces or making premises available for new businesses.

National contacts
Business in the Community (target teams for Local Purchasing and Finance for Enterprise).

Local contacts
Chambers of Commerce; the Government's City Action Teams and inner city Task Forces; enterprise agencies; TECs and LECs.

Investment in urban renewal
Companies can help to make inner cities and other disadvantaged areas more attractive to business and to residents by developing land for housing and business property; by locating offices and factories in inner city areas; by contributing to environmental improvements in inner cities and urban fringes.

National contacts
Association of British Chambers of Commerce; British Urban Regeneration Association; Business in the Community; Confederation of British Industry; Department of the Environment; Groundwork Foundation; the Phoenix Initiative.

Local contacts
Chambers of Commerce; the Government's City Action Teams and inner city Task Forces; Groundwork Trusts; local authority economic development units; Urban Development Corporations.

Partnership ventures
Companies can develop effective partnership initiatives for community action with organisations from private, public and voluntary sectors. The partnership approach is especially relevant to urban renewal activities and to inner city training and employment ventures.

National contacts
Association of British Chambers of Commerce; Business in the Community (for details of Business Leadership Teams); Common Purpose (special training for partnership – and network-building between leaders from different sectors); Community Projects Foundation; Confederation of British Industry.

Local contacts
Business Leadership Teams; Chambers of Commerce; the Government's City Action Teams and inner city Task Forces; local authority economic development units; TECs and LECs.

Appendix 3

Oganisations to contact

The organisations listed below can all offer information, expertise and advice on different aspects of business investment in the community.

Business and voluntary sector agencies

Action Match
Action Match is a specialist voluntary agency promoting business sponsorship of social causes. It provides training, advice and consultancy on social sponsorship and acts as a broker between companies and community organisations looking for sponsorship opportunities.

Contact
Mandy Wilson, Director, Action Match, Aizlewoods Mill, Nursery Street, Sheffield S3 8GG
Telephone: 0742-823163

Action Resource Centre (ARC)
ARC is the leading agency specialising in secondments to voluntary organisations. ARC provides advice and consultancy to companies and the public sector on secondment practice and a brokerage service to manage secondee placements. Secondments may be full-time or part-time, and short-term assignments are also offered, designed to enhance secondees' management skills as well as provide benefit to community organisations.

Contact
John Uden, Development Director, Action Resource Centre, First Floor, 102 Park Village East, London NW1 3SP
Telephone: 071-383 2200

Association of British Chambers of Commerce (ABCC)
Chambers of Commerce are representative bodies for local business and are active in many areas in promoting business involvement in the community. Chambers frequently work in partnership with other private

and public sector organisations in fields such as business-education links, training initiatives, enterprise support and urban renewal initiatives.

Contact
Association of British Chambers of Commerce, Sovereign House, 212 Shaftesbury Avenue, London WC2H 8EW
Telephone: 071-240 5831

British Urban Regeneration Association (BURA)

BURA, founded in 1990, is an association of organisations in the private, public and voluntary sectors involved in urban renewal and development. It aims to provide a forum for policy debate, information exchange and dissemination of good practice in urban renewal projects.

Contact
BURA, 33 Great Sutton Street, London EC1V 0DX
Telephone: 071-253 5054

Business in the Community (BitC)

BitC was founded in 1981 by industry in partnership with government, the voluntary sector and the trade unions in order to promote community involvement by business. BitC is supported by over 400 of the UK's leading companies and its members also include representatives of government departments, voluntary agencies and trade unions.

Business in the Community promotes the benefits to all parties of business involvement in community initiatives and offers advice and consultancy on corporate policy to companies seeking to develop strategies for practical action. BitC is the coordinating body for the national network of enterprise agencies; it oversees the development of Business Leadership Teams, partnerships between local business leaders and public sector and community agencies; and it coordinates the national and local Per Cent Clubs, which aim to encourage higher levels of community contributions by business.

Contact
Chief Executive, Business in the Community, 227a City Road, London EC1V 1LX
Telephone: 071-253 3716

Charities Aid Foundation (CAF)

CAF acts as a channel for tax-efficient charitable giving by companies and individuals, and promotes company giving through publications, policy advice and the GIVE AS YOU EARN payroll giving scheme, which it oversees.

Contact:
Charities Aid Foundation, 48 Pembury Road, Tonbridge, Kent TN9 2JD
Telephone: 0732-771333

Common Purpose
Common Purpose develops training programmes designed to bring together leading representatives of private, public and voluntary sector organisations in particular cities. The aim of Common Purpose programmes is to promote increased mutual understanding among leaders from different walks of life and help to develop effective networks and partnerships between them. Common Purpose schemes were piloted in the UK in Newcastle and Coventry, and many other towns and cities are now involved in the initiative.

Contact
Julia Middleton, Chief Executive, Common Purpose, 12-18 Hoxton Street, London N1 6NG
Telephone: 071-729 5979

Community Development Foundation (CDF)
CDF is an agency working in partnership with local authorities and business on a wide variety of community regeneration projects. It offers consultancy and training on community development projects and business involvement in the community. It has devised a Community Investment Charter, launched in Spring 1991 with the support of leading companies.

Contact
Chief Executive, Community Development Foundation, 60 Highbury Grove, London N5 2AG
Telephone: 071-226 5375

Confederation of British Industry (CBI)
The CBI works with Business in the Community and the Phoenix Initiative in promoting the involvement of companies in the economic and social regeneration of Britain's cities. It also promotes education-industry links.

Contact
Director General, Confederation of British Industry, Centre Point, 103 New Oxford Street, London WC1A 1DU
Telephone: 071-379 7400

Council for Industry and Higher Education (CIHE)
CIHE is an independent body which brings together heads of major companies and heads of universities, polytechnics and higher education colleges. Its aim is to promote partnership between industry and higher education and represent their joint thinking to government.

Contact
Patrick Coldstream, Director, Council for Industry and Higher Education, 100 Park Village East, London NW1 3SR
Telephone: 071-387 2171

Directory of Social Change (DSC)
An independent charity providing advice, information and training to the voluntary sector and consultancy and information to business on developing policies for community involvement. DSC publishes the biannual *Guide to Company Giving and the Corporate Donor's Handbook.*

Contact
Directory of Social Change, Radius Works, Back Lane,
London NW3 1HL
Telephone: 071-435 8171

Fullemploy Group
Formerly known as Project Fullemploy, the Fullemploy Group is a voluntary sector agency working on initiatives to improve training and employment opportunities for ethnic minority communities in the UK. Fullemploy works in partnership with other voluntary bodies, with public agencies and with businesses.

Contact
Fullemploy Group, County House, 190 Great Dover Street,
London SE1 4YB
Telephone: 071-378 1774

Groundwork Foundation
The Groundwork Foundation was established as a national charity in 1985 following the success of the network of local Groundwork Trusts, through which business, public agencies and voluntary bodies work in partnership on environmental improvement projects in and around urban areas. The Foundation coordinates the work of the local trusts and promotes business sponsorship of environmental projects.

Contact
Groundwork Foundation, Bennetts Court, 6 Bennetts Hill,
Birmingham B2 5ST
Telephone: 021-236 8565

Industrial Society
The Industrial Society provides advice and training on personnel and other
management issues and is involved in many partnership initiatives in areas
such as targeted training, education-industry links and training for the
voluntary sector. It has a specialist Inner Cities Unit working on the
development of community initiatives in urban areas.

Contact
Jeremy Thorn, Divisional Director, The Industrial Society, Robert Hyde
House, 48 Bryanston Square, London W1H 7LN
Telephone: 071-262 2401

Institute of Personnel Management (IPM)
The IPM is the professional personnel management organisation in the UK,
with a membership of over 40,000. It is involved in promoting partnership
initiatives between business, the public sector and the community in
relation to targeted employment, education links and customised training
in the inner cities.

Contact
Organisation & Human Resource Planning Manager, Institute of
Personnel Management, IPM House, 35 Camp Road, London SW19 4UX
Telephone: 081-946 9100

National Council for Voluntary Organisations (NCVO)
NCVO is the national agency representing and promoting the voluntary
sector, and can provide information and advice on working with charities
and other community organisations.

Contact
National Council for Voluntary Organisations, 26 Bedford Square,
London WC1B 3HJ
Telephone: 071-636 4066

National Youth Agency
The National Youth Agency was set up as a national youth service body in
April 1991, bringing together existing national bodies, to work with both
the voluntary and local authority sectors of the Youth Service. The Agency
undertakes a range of education-related functions, particularly in the areas

of accrediting and validating youth worker and management training. It also gives direct support to government initiatives in these areas.

Contact
Janet Paraskeva, Director, 17-23 Albion Street, Leicester LE1 6GC
Telephone: 0533-471200

The Per Cent Club

The Per Cent Club is a group of leading companies that have committed themselves to contributing up to 1 per cent of pre-tax profits to the community in the form of cash donations, gifts in kind and other types of support such as secondments. Local Per Cent Clubs have been set up in Newcastle and Sheffield. Information on the Clubs is available from Business in the Community, which provides the secretariat for the Per Cent Club.

Contact
The Per Cent Club, c/o Business in the Community, 227a City Road,
London EC1V 1LX
Telephone: 071-253 3716

Phoenix Initiative

The Phoenix Initiative is a non-profit organisation specialising in urban regeneration. It provides advice and information on aspects of urban renewal, and also works as a catalyst within inner cities, bringing representatives of organisations from business and other sectors into partnership ventures.

Contact
Chief Executive, The Phoenix Initiative, 26 Store Street,
London WC1E 7BT
Telephone: 071-436 1561

UK 2000

UK 2000 is an environmental initiative bringing together the six main national voluntary organisations concerned with environmental improvement in partnership with government and the private sector. The six member organisations carry out projects, foster business awareness, secure sponsorship and provide training opportunities for the unemployed. The six members are: British Trust for Conservation Volunteers, Civic Trust, Community Service Volunteers, Friends of the Earth, Groundwork Foundation and Royal Society for Nature Conservation.

Contact
Rebecca Rendle, Publicity Officer, UK2000/Community Service
Volunteers, 237 Pentonville Road, London N1 9NJ
Telephone: 071-278 6601

Volunteers
Volunteers is for young people aged 16-24. It provides them with an
opportunity for personal development by joining a team with others from
different backgrounds/walks of life and undertaking a period of voluntary
work in the community.

Contact
The Director, Volunteers, 8 Jockeys Fields, London WC1R 4JT
Telephone: 071-430 0378

Volunteer Centre UK
The Volunteer Centre is the national agency coordinating the network of
local volunteer bureaux and promoting volunteering in the community. The
Volunteer Centre can offer advice and information on volunteering
schemes for company employees and retirees.

Contact
The Director, The Volunteer Centre UK, 29 Lower Kings Road,
Berkhamsted, Herts. HP4 2AB
Telephone: 0442-873311

Government departments and public agencies
Government measures for the development of urban renewal initiatives and
partnerships between public and private sector organisations and
community bodies are coordinated within the ACTION FOR CITIES
initiative. This brings together different government departments and
public agencies with a role in urban regeneration. The main contact points
for companies wishing to find out more about Action For Cities are listed
below.

City Action Teams (CATs)
CATs coordinate the action of different departments at local level in major
urban areas and are a central contact point for businesses and for voluntary
bodies and community organisations.

Contact CAT secretaries or leaders on
Birmingham   021-631 6042
Cleveland   0642-226166
Leeds/Bradford   0532-438232
Liverpool   051-227 4111
London   071-278 0363
Manchester/Salford   061-833 0251
Nottingham/Derby/Leicester   0602-506181
Tyne & Wear   091-232 4722

Department of the Environment (DoE)
The DoE coordinates the government's inner city activities and runs several urban renewal initiatives aimed at attracting private sector investment to inner cities and developing local authority schemes for regeneration. DoE initiatives include Urban Development Corporations, City Grant, Derelict Land Grant, Enterprise Zones, Estate Action and the Urban Programme. DoE has eight regional offices.

Contact
Action for Cities Coordinating Unit: 071-276-3053

Urban Development Corporations (UDCs)
The eleven UDCs promote private sector investment for regeneration of designated urban areas.

UDC contacts
Black Country   021-552 4200
Bristol   0272-218804
Cardiff Bay   0222-471576
Central Manchester   061-236 1166
Leeds   0532-46273
London Docklands   071-512 3000
Merseyside   051-236 6090
Sheffield   0742-720100
Teeside   0642-230636
Trafford Park (Manchester)   061-648 8000
Tyne & Wear   091-222 1222

Department of Trade and Industry (DTI)
The DTI runs the Inner City TASK FORCES, which work in localities with particularly severe problems. The Task Forces work with local businesses

and community groups to promote initiatives on training, employment and business start-ups. Task Forces currently in operation are listed below.

Contacts

Birmingham (East)	021-326 7005
Bradford	0274-542222
Bristol	0272-550205
Coventry	0203-631855
Derby	0332-298800
Hartlepool	0429-860557
Leeds (Chapletown/Harehills)	0532-626202
Liverpool (Granby/Toxteth)	051-734 5289
Manchester (Moss Side/Hulme)	061-226 8899
Middlesbrough	0642-300420
Nottingham	0602-421565
Wirral	051-653 4515

London area Task Forces:

Deptford	071-694 9276
W. London	071-960 8455
N. Peckham	081-358 9018
Spitalfields	071-375 1163

Inner Cities Central Unit:
1 Victoria Street
London SW1H 0E   071-215 4557

Employment Department Group
The Employment Department oversees all training and enterprise initiatives and school/industry Compact schemes which are now being managed by the local TRAINING AND ENTERPRISE COUNCILS (TECs) in England and Wales and by LOCAL ENTERPRISE COMPANIES (LECs) in Scotland. These initiatives include Employment Training, Youth Training, Enterprise Allowance and the Small Firms Service. The Department also oversees the EMPLOYMENT SERVICE, which operates the Jobcentre network and is involved in many local initiatives to promote training and job opportunities.

Contact for information on the national TEC network
TEC Branch, Training, Enterprise & Education Directorate
Employment Department Group, Moorfoot, Sheffield S1 4PQ
Telephone: 0742-753275

For enquiries on urban regeneration outside England

Scotland
Urban Policy Division 2
Industry Department for Scotland
New St Andrew's House, Edinburgh EH1 3TA
Telephone: 031-244 2062

Wales
Urban Affairs
Welsh Office
Cathays Park, Cardiff CF1 3NQ
Telephone: 0222-823633

Northern Ireland
Belfast Development Office
DoE (Northern Ireland)
Clarendon House, 9-21 Adelaide Street, Belfast BT2 8NR
Telephone: 0232-244300 ext.2394

Appendix 4

Bibliography

Association of British Chambers of Commerce, *A Tale of Four Cities: business responsibility in action*, London: ABCC, 1989

Audit Commission, *Urban Regeneration and Economic Development: the local government dimension*, London: HMSO, 1989

Business in the Cities, *Leadership in the Community: a blueprint for business involvement in the 1990s*, London: Business in the Community, 1990

Business in the Community, *Agenda for Action*, London: BitC, 1990

Business in the Community, *Springboard for Growth*, London: BitC, 1991

M. Carley, *Housing and Neighbourhood Renewal: Britain's new urban challenge*, London: Policy Studies Institute, 1990

I. Christie, *Profitable Partnerships: an action guide for company investment in the community*, London: Policy Studies Institute, 1991

Community Projects Foundation, *Signposts to Community Action: a guide for business*, London: CPF, 1989

Confederation of British Industry (CBI), *Initiatives Beyond Charity: report of the CBI Task Force on business and urban regeneration*, London: CBI, 1988

Council for Industry and Higher Education (CIHE), *Towards a Partnership: the company response*, London: CIHE, 1988

T. Crowley-Bainton and M. White, *Employing Unemployed People: how employers gain*, London: HMSO, 1990

E. Crowther-Hunt and L. Billinghurst, *Inner Cities, Inner Strengths: recognising people potential in urban regeneration*, London: Industrial Society Press, 1990

Department of the Environment, *Developing Businesses: case studies of good practice in urban regeneration*, London: HMSO, 1988

Department of the Environment, *Community Businesses: case studies of good practice in urban regeneration*, London: HMSO, 1990

Department of the Environment, *Getting People into Jobs: good practice in urban regeneration*, London: HMSO, 1990

Department of the Environment, *People in Cities*, London: HMSO, 1990

Department of the Environment, *Targeting Urban Employment Initiatives*, London: HMSO, 1990

Department of Trade and Industry, *Customised Training: lessons from the Inner Cities Initiative*, London: DTI, 1990

Ernst and Young, *Companies and the Community: a report on West Midlands links*, London: Department of Trade and Industry, 1990

M. Fogarty and I. Christie, *Companies and Communities: promoting business involvement in the community*, London: Policy Studies Institute, 1991

S. Forrester, *Business and Environmental Groups – a natural partnership?*, London: Directory of Social Change, 1990

R. Hambleton, 'Privatising urban regeneration', *Town & County Planning*, November 1990, vol. 59, no.11

H. Metcalf, R. Pearson and R. Martin, *Stimulating Jobs: the charitable role of companies*, Brighton: Institute of Manpower Studies, 1989

M. Norton, *The Corporate Donor's Guide*, London: Directory of Social Change, 1987

M. Norton, *A Guide to Company Giving*, London: Directory of Social Change, 1991

Segal Quince Wickstead, *Encouraging Small Business Start-Up and Growth*, London: HMSO, 1988